T0323707

Cambridge Elements ≡

Elements in Translation and Interpreting
edited by
Kirsten Malmkjær
University of Leicester

TRANSLATION AS CREATIVE-CRITICAL PRACTICE

Delphine Grass
Lancaster University

CAMBRIDGE
UNIVERSITY PRESS

CAMBRIDGE
UNIVERSITY PRESS

Shaftesbury Road, Cambridge CB2 8EA, United Kingdom

One Liberty Plaza, 20th Floor, New York, NY 10006, USA

477 Williamstown Road, Port Melbourne, VIC 3207, Australia

314–321, 3rd Floor, Plot 3, Splendor Forum, Jasola District Centre, New Delhi – 110025, India

103 Penang Road, #05–06/07, Visioncrest Commercial, Singapore 238467

Cambridge University Press is part of Cambridge University Press & Assessment, a department of the University of Cambridge.

We share the University's mission to contribute to society through the pursuit of education, learning and research at the highest international levels of excellence.

www.cambridge.org
Information on this title: www.cambridge.org/9781009462556

DOI: 10.1017/9781009075039

First published 2023

A catalogue record for this publication is available from the British Library

ISBN 978-1-009-46255-6 Hardback
ISBN 978-1-009-07483-4 Paperback
ISSN 2633-6480 (online)
ISSN 2633-6472 (print)

Cambridge University Press & Assessment has no responsibility for the persistence or accuracy of URLs for external or third-party internet websites referred to in this publication and does not guarantee that any content on such websites is, or will remain, accurate or appropriate.

Translation as Creative–Critical Practice

Elements in Translation and Interpreting

DOI: 10.1017/9781009075039
First published online: November 2023

Delphine Grass
Lancaster University

Author for correspondence: Delphine Grass, d.grass@lancaster.ac.uk

Abstract: In *Translation as Creative-Critical Practice*, Delphine Grass questions the separation between practice and theory in translation studies through her analysis of creative-critical translation experiments. Focusing on contemporary literary and artistic engagements with translation such as the autotheoretical translation memoir, performative translations and 'transtopian' literary and visual art works, this study argues for a renewed engagement with translation theory from the point of view of translation as artistic and practice-based research capable of reframing translation theory. Exploring examples of translation as both a norm-breaking and world-making activity in the works of Kate Briggs, Ayesha Manazir Siddiqi, Noémie Grunenwald, Anne Carson, Charles Bernstein, Chantal Wright or Slavs and Tatars to name a few, this Element prompts us to reconsider the current place of translation practice in translation studies.

Keywords: translation, literature, creative-critical writing, autotheory, performativity

ISBNs: 9781009462556 (HB), 9781009074834 (PB), 9781009075039 (OC)
ISSNs: 2633-6480 (online), 2633-6472 (print)

Contents

Introduction

During a conference I organised in 2017 entitled 'The Space in Between: Thinking Translation in Creation', Elise Aru presented a series of translation sculptures of twentieth-century French surrealist poems which she invited us to manipulate. The fragile quality of the boxes and the material support used for their content (a bandage, a puzzle, a glass jar . . .) meant that we had to take great care in opening, touching and unravelling the translation-objects they contained (Aru 2017). Hers were translations which required that we, as critics and scholars, adapt, move and contort our bodies in relation to the material with which we were trying to engage. Transformed by contact with Aru's object-translations, our mode of engagement with her works became, de facto, an enterprise of touch and tactfulness: our point of entry in analysing them was dependent on our point of contact with the objects. Aru's work taught us something important about the relationship between translation and critique that I want to continue to explore in this work: the possibility of approaching translation theory from the point of view of translation practice as a materially situated and critically engaged meaning-making process, of exploring how experimenting with translation could invite fixed forms of theory into a space of experimental possibilities. This study is an attempt to deconstruct the relationship between theory and practice in translation studies by exploring translation practices as a form of critical thinking on the nature of translation. Rather than an afterthought, or a preventative measure applied to practice, it argues that translation theory is something which can be analysed and critiqued in and through translation as a form of creative-critical performance. It asks: what forms of critical thinking happen in translation? What happens when ethical concerns and political commentaries are performed and addressed in translation practice? The performative and at times tactile dimension of creative-critical translation practices, I want to argue in this work, can bring to our consciousness the ways in which theory and criticism touch and translate their objects, but also invite us to reconsider the nature and function of translation beyond interlingual communication.

As a discipline, translation studies has traditionally been organised around a stark separation between theory and practice. One way to situate translation practice and theory in the discipline of translation studies might be to consider translation practice's temporal relation to translation theory. Where, and when, does translation theory traditionally take place in the field of academic translation studies? How can we map translation theory temporally in relation to practice? Although much of twentieth-century translation theory has been written by translators, translation theory has traditionally been located outside of practice in our mental maps of translation studies and not in the here and now of 'doing' translation. Today, the disciplinary relationship between translation practice and theory remains largely mapped along separate temporal lines: theory is either what happens before or after translation through close-reading analysis. Advising 'applied translation' from a distance, its role was either to mould it through a form of pre-emptive self-awareness thought to be lacking from translation practice or to retroactively analyse translation norms and methods of exporting or importing cultures.

The demotion of the here and now of translation practice as peripherally anecdotal to stronger theories of translation is well illustrated by Holmes' highly influential translation studies map. To this day, this framework remains central to translation studies learning, and highlights the disciplinary gap perceived between what Holmes names 'pure theory' and 'applied translation' (Holmes 1972), as visually illustrated in Gideon Toury's representation of these concepts (Figure 1).

This disciplinary map of translation studies features no apparent pathways or links between translation theory and practice. While 'applied' translation suggests the unmediated application of translation methods and linguistic procedures, only descriptive and theoretical approaches are admitted to what Holmes named 'Pure' translation studies. The 'translation criticism' sub-branch, meanwhile, describes the a-posteriori critique of translated texts in an editorial context. No thinking, no theorising, then, is thought to happen 'in translation'; theory remains pure and removed from the critical stammering of translation practice as a form of linguistic production. More maps have been created since Holmes' (see Hatim and Munday 2004; Snell-Hornby 2006; van Doorslaer

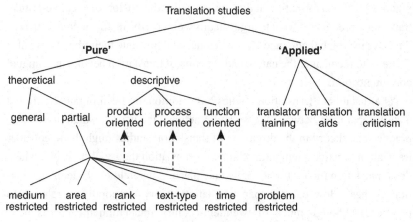

Figure 1 Holmes' 'map' of translation studies (Toury 1995: 10)

2007; Vandepitte 2008; Chesterman 2009; Pym 2014), and Chesterman and Wagner's *Can Theory Help Translators?* has made inroads by questioning the relevance of theory in the context of translation practice (2002). That said, aside from Jeremy Munday's pertinent critique of 'the artificial gap between practice and theory', there has, until the emergence of the 'creative turn', been little attempt at bridging theory and practice in the field of translation studies (Loffredo and Perteghella 2006; Munday 2016: 26).

This Element aims to address this disparity by exploring approaches to translation criticism and translation theory which I call 'creative critical'. Creative-critical writing is a burgeoning field at the crossroads between research and creative practice which seeks to use a wide range of genres and media to engage with writing about art and literature. Bringing criticism and creativity closer together, it fosters an innovative approach to literary and art criticism by rethinking the conventions of the scholarly output, intending for creative writing to be an integral part of the critical process, and vice versa (Benson and Connors 2014; Felski 2015; Hilvaara and Orley 2018; Mussgnug, Nabugodi and Petrou 2021). Since the process of translation requires both critical distantiation from and artistic engagement with its source text, literary translation is naturally at the crossroads between creative writing and criticism. Theorising *from* practice or *in* practice rather than *about* it from a distance, the works I will explore perform translation in literary and artistic forms in a way that often challenges the underlying assumptions legitimating translation norms of transparency and equivalence, as well as the relationship between originals and translations, source text and target text. If creative-critical translation can be a method of practicing theory which poetically adapts to the contours of the object and subject of critique, it can be argued that it is also an experimental approach to translation practice as a method of research into wider theoretical concepts pertaining to translation equivalence and the differences between languages and cultures.

To some extent, creative-critical translations propose to abandon the relationship of authority between practice and theory in order to adopt a more multidimensional approach to translation as an epistemological field. This study uses the term 'creativity' to refer to norm-breaking aesthetic innovations in translation and argues that artistic experimentations with translation practice can lead to theoretical insights into the nature of translation beyond its communicative framework. In this sense, creativity and criticism in creative-critical practices can be said to intentionally overlap, and it is this 'jamming' of traditionally separate terms of engagements with translation I am interested in putting to work. How does breaking away from traditional translation practices through formal innovation help us reassess and question translation norms and the ideologies which underpin them? I argue that multimodal and creative-writing translation experiments can be used to engage critically with translation theory and criticism in ways more conventional forms of academic writing might not be able to do. Conversely, by materialising language through translation, translation as creative-critical practice extends the material textures of creative-critical practice beyond writing and authorship as traditionally understood.

The epistemological value of such an expansion of creative practice in translation studies has already been successfully demonstrated by, for example, Madeleine Campbell and Ricarda Vidal in their intersemiotic approach to translation. In their work 'The Translator's Gaze: Intersemiotic Translation as Transactional Process', they show, for example, that 'intersemiotic translation allows non-verbal aspects of human thought and affect to take expressive forms that arise from common conceptual mechanisms for meaning-making and embodied cognition' (Campbell and Vidal 2019: 5). Similarly, in their careful examination of the creative turn in translation studies, Manuela Perteghella and Eugenia Loffredo demonstrate that creativity, 'perceived in a multiplicity of modes and expressions that accommodate its many functions and directions', can widen our understanding of translation as a cognitive process (Loffredo and Perteghella 2006: 11). In this study, I argue that multimodal engagements with translation practice can also participate in the theorisation of translation in the etymological sense by allowing us to view, consider, and examine translation from different angles and positions. At the same time, my understanding of creative-critical practice rests on the intuition that creativity in translation without criticism can easily run the risk of reproducing forms of symbolic violence, coloniality and appropriation if not approached with enough critical care. Instead, the creative critical questions the separation between translation practice and translation theory from the perspective of translation as a world-making, politically situated and socially imaginative enterprise.

Far from fostering uncritical and unethical models of creativity in translation, then, I put forward creative-critical translation practice as a way of interrogating the histories and ideologies embedded in the traditional separation between theory and practice in translation studies. By analysing texts and visual art works which provoke us into rethinking our theoretical assumptions about translation, my aim is to glimpse what translation as a form of practice-led and embodied research might look and *think* like, and to encourage us to invite these works into our understanding of translation as an epistemological and pedagogical field of learning. Moreover, I am hoping that this study will encourage a rethink of translation criticism, positioning it more broadly as a creative and critical transcultural process. Rather than accepting and performing within pre-existing, stable definitions of cultural and linguistic differences, the works I will explore seek to create new frameworks of understanding on the creative geographies of translation as a spatially critical enterprise. Indeed, translation not only operates between spaces but creates, transforms, and performs new spaces and contexts in the performative act of translating.

Lawrence Venuti and Douglas Robinson have recently eloquently troubled instrumental models of translation (Venuti 2019; Robinson 2022). Robinson, whose works on the somatics of translation in *The Translator's Turn* (Robinson 1991) opened translation practice to metacognitive fields of enquiry, made the convincing case that instrumentalist views of translation prevent us from experimenting with translation as a creative enterprise in its own right (Robinson 2022). Robinson and Venuti's anti-instrumentalist stances echo the works of many scholars who have redefined the relationship between translation and creative writing in recent years. Cecilia Rossi's 'Translation as a Creative Force', for example, advocates for greater focus on literary translation practice as a creative, and therefore, performative process (Rossi 2018). Her analysis echoes Susan Bassnett's resistance to distinguishing between writing and translating in her essay 'Writing and Translating' (Bassnett 2008). In it, Bassnett decries the lack of value granted to translation practice as research at an institutional level, lamenting the fact that scholars are discouraged from listing their translations as 'serious' publications (Bassnett 2008: 173). While these works do not necessarily address the boundary between theory and practice in translation studies, they edge closer to a comprehensive description of literary translation processes by demystifying the distinction between writing and translating, lending content, weight and complexity to what is still largely approached, in contrast to creative writing, as a purely mimetic transaction.

A growing number of contemporary scholars have explored how multimodal approaches to translation can deepen our understanding of translation processes (Johnston 2013; Campbell and Vidal 2019; Bennett 2020; Vidal Claramonte 2022), while others have advocated for innovation in translation practice itself. In his seminal *Literary Translation and the Rediscovery of Reading*, Clive Scott experiments with phenomenological approaches to translation as a meaning-making activity. Through his practice-based approach to texts, Scott uses translation practice 'to argue that translation should encourage the reader of a source text (ST) to write his/her responses, his/her own particular insights and associations ...so that the TT can be seen as the ST re-textualised, given new expressive coordinates, in the here and now of the reading act' (Scott 2012: 187). Scott, however, does not explore the productive relations between creativity and criticism in this context: 'It will be apparent that I do not imagine any neat reconciliation of critical and creative principles. The ends they serve are, for me, all but diametrically opposed. But the creative will inevitably build on the critical' (Scott 2021: 205). Here Scott makes it clear that his experimental practice does not aim to serve a critical purpose. As an experiment in self-creativity and transformation, his creative translation practice remains unconcerned by wider theoretical considerations of the ethics and politics of translating particular texts in particular contexts. My approach differs in that I am interested in how creative-critical translation practices challenge the theories reproduced in translational norms. I therefore read experimental translation practices in the context of wider political struggles of legitimacy in the context of gender and post-colonial relations, which, I argue, are reinforced in the very division between practice and theory in the field of translation studies.

Further to these texts, recent conceptual approaches to translation practice as a hermeneutic activity come close to my understanding of translation as creative-critical practice (Aru 2010; Kadiu 2019; Venuti 2019; Malmkjær 2020; Robert-Foley 2020; Batchelor 2022 and Lee 2022). Kadiu's *Reflexive Translation Studies: Translation as Critical Reflection* practises a form of theorising which 'takes place during the translating process itself, in the act of undertaking a translation and attempting to articulate our experience of it, of facing a translation dilemma and reflecting on possible solutions' (viii). Her astute reflexive translations of translation theories reveal the critical input which goes into all translation processes and how they may inform wider theoretical frameworks of translation. Kathryn Batchelor's 'Translation as Commentary' also recently analysed how translation can serve as a form of commentary or literary criticism (Batchelor 2022). Robert-Foley's article 'The Politics of Experimental Translation: Potentialities and Preoccupations', meanwhile, is an illuminating study into the relationship between linguistic equivalence and questions of social justice (Robert-Foley 2020). Starting from the 'belief that the structures of aesthetics and poetics are profoundly and radically political', Robert-Foley deconstructs the notion of equivalence in translation norms from the perspective of experimental translation practice (Robert-Foley 405). Her critique is expanded in *Experimental Translation: The Work of Translation in the Age of Algorithmic Production*, in which she explains that 'the critique of norms in experimental translation is profoundly situated, in its language, its cultural and historical specificity' (Robert-Foley, in press).

Like Robert-Foley's, my exploration of translation as creative-critical practice is concerned with questions of social justice and representation beyond translation theory. Like all linguistic practices, I argue that meaning making in translation takes place within wide networks of social relations which translation practices and norms both reproduce and manipulate (Bourdieu 1973; Hermans 1996). Underwriting my exploration of the relationship between practice and theory in translation studies is Naoki Sakai's reframing of translation as what creates and stabilises differences between languages, rather than what bridges differences (Sakai 2017). As I will show, creative-critical translation practices resist the classification of cultures and languages which 'the modern regime of translation' reproduces (Sakai 2017). In this study, I therefore also propose to analyse the hierarchical relationship between translation practice and theory as a stabilising force of social and geographical norms. My Element posits that the apparent division of labour between practice and theory in translation studies is not socially neutral but reproduces wider asymmetries of power along the lines of gender, racial and social inequalities by perpetuating silence and ways of (not) listening to the theoretical thinking implied in conventional and unconventional translation choices. In other words, I argue that to open translation to creative-critical enquiry is to move away from a communicative model of translation in order to reframe and rethink the regime of translation which naturalises such differences.

Section 1 discusses how the division between practice and theory in translation studies comes under scrutiny in what I call 'autotheoretical' translation memoirs. Predominantly written by women, autotheoretical translation memoirs explore translation as an embodied experience of the relationship between practice and theory in translation. They can be interpreted as a wider critique of strong theory's inclination to overlook the 'tender things' of translation (Siddiqi 2022), and its tendency to underestimate the entangled and co-emergent relation between language and matter in processes of theorisation (Barad 2007). Section 2 explores what I call performative translations, or translations which make visible and question the performativity present in translation as a repetition of norms, differences and values, as well as texts. After exploring the theoretical contours of performative translation practice by analysing experimental translations by Charles Berstein, Caroline Bergvall, and Erin Moure, this analysis focuses on Anne Carson's translation of Sappho's texts. I analyse how the practice of translation itself is mobilised in her performance of interpretation and theorisation. The third and final Section focuses on visual and literary examples of what I call 'transtopian' translations, or translations which explore and disrupt geopolitical frameworks of identity modelled on the nation. Instead of 'thickening' the source-text or culture in translation, I argue that transtopian approaches to translation 'thicken' the practice of translation itself as a location of critique and contestation of hegemonic ontologies of belonging (Appiah 1993).

1 The Translation Memoir as Autotheory

At the beginning of her translation memoir *Traduire ou perdre pied* (*To Translate or to Lose one's Footing*, my translation, 2019), Corinna Gepner recalls her disappointment at encountering Dostoevsky's works in a different translation than the one she had first read. She situates this moment in time and place, accompanied by a description of the feelings emerging from this discovery: 'One day, after realising I had forgotten my book, I went to borrow another copy from the high-school library at break time. I did not recognise the text. My disappointment was so strong that I had to stop reading. I could no longer find what I had liked in it' (Gepner 2019: 9, my translation).

The reader is then offered three different translations of an extract from Dostoevsky's *Crime and Punishment*. Gepner appears to invite a comparison between the three Dostoevsky translations, but does not undertake it; nor does she reveal which of the three was her favourite. Perhaps the reader will take up this task, perhaps not. What happens through this not taking place is that the door of analysis remains ajar, like a question: how should one approach such a comparison *anyway*? But also: why does one become emotionally attached to one translation above others? Then, the beginning of a theory emerges:

> Through every translation, I hear something unique. Together, they almost form a concert of voices which, though emerging from the same trunk, expand their branches. None is more, nor less, beautiful than the other. It is probably wrong to think that literary works can only be written once. Through translation, they are rewritten with a difference, and every translation is but another rewriting which cannot ignore the others. The first literary work to appear is only the tangible manifestation of the beginning of writing. If so, what do I translate? (Gepner 2019: 25, my translation)

This passage in Gepner's text consists of a critical reflection on translation as a form of writing which can be contrasted with traditional translation criticism in more than one way: de-authorised and plural, translation is theorised from the perspective of translation practice, rather than in relation to the source text. Gepner's narrative focuses on the relationship between translator and translation, rather than on the relationship between the translation and the source text. Rather than comparing the translations to determine which is closest to the intentions of the original, Gepner chooses instead to stay a little longer with the affective troubles of translating. What transpires in this deceptively personal, or individual, theory of translation is a proposition which, if taken seriously, has the potential to challenge the artificial limit between not only translation and writing but translation practice and translation theory. Gepner not only questions whether it is ever possible to theorise about translation in general, abstract terms, but argues that the division between creative writing and criticism is artificially maintained by a false dichotomy between writing and rewriting.

Throughout her translation memoir, the time and place of Gepner's insights are represented and described as part of a wider network of material clues and sensations: the college, the library, her adolescent illusions about literature, all are elements attended to, taken seriously, as it were, as the stuff (etymologically, the 'material', the 'furniture', that which 'pads' and, crucially, 'draws together') that *matters* to her thinking on translation. Both the stuff of writing and reading translations, in other words, the practices in and around translation, become her thinking about translation as well as its object. Gepner's critical insights are not presented as a definitive vision of what translation is or should be, but rather, her interest and thinking on translation is staged as an encounter, a meeting that takes place at a particular time and place in her personal history as a reader of translations who decides, one day, to do translations herself. This is a text at once biographical and philosophical, one in which not a single overarching theoretical framework emerges, but in which many small, at times seemingly transient theories of doing and thinking translation surface and remain entangled in the first-person singular. In doing so, Gepner is able to draw on the strength of the 'weak' but living ties between doing translation and thinking about translation theoretically.

This form of theorising translation which does not petrify its object into a definitive version is what interests me here in the autotheoretical translation memoir as a counterpoint to other ways of *doing* translation theory: I am talking about a practice-led approach to translation theory in which theorising remains open to the twists and turns of its practice, an experiment in thinking with translation rather than a straightforward synthetisation of its craft. In his illuminating 'Notes on Translating the Self', Paschalis Nikolaou convincingly argued that, 'the clandestine self-translations which impel creativity in both original and translation . . . produce literary spaces in between' (Nikolaou 2006: 20). Taking inspiration from Nikolaou's 'autoscopic' translation approach and other creative-critical engagements with theory in literature and the arts, this section will focus on the theoretical potential nestled in such creative forms of translation (Nikolaou 2006: 29). In the following sections, I will introduce and use the concept of autotheory quite loosely, mapping what I call the moments of theorisation which are enabled by the translation memoir as a method in textual and self-translation, and therefore autotheorisation. My focus will be to explore how the translation memoir thickens not the translation but the material networks and power relations underpinning translation as a cultural, embodied practice. Instead of yielding strong theoretical claims, I will argue that the translation memoir engages with what Eve Kosofsky Sedgwick (1997) and Kathleen Stewart (2008), among others, describe as 'weak' theory, that is, as forms of knowledge which do not prescribe themselves to the reader in a totalising fashion but attempt to put practice, social experience and theory into productive discussion. I choose to retain the term 'memoir' because, rather than a complete rupture with the memoir as a genre and mode of self-inquiry, I see these works as questioning the social and material nature of translation practice through the subjective and temporal node of provisionality and partiality offered by traditional memoir writing. Playing, subverting and breaking down the boundaries between the essay and the memoir makes it possible for translators to interrogate their subject positions in the epistemological field of translation. This form of writing, then, allows them to sidestep current epistemic maps of translation and overcome the dichotomy between theory and practice. As a figuration of the translating 'I', the autotheoretical translation memoir makes it possible to inaugurate new subject positions of critical enunciation outside of more omniscient academic forms of writing.

While many twentieth-century memoirists often used translation as a metaphor to describe diasporic and transnational experiences (Karpinsky 2012), the contemporary translation memoirs I will focus on constitute a form of theoretical engagement with translation practice both as a form of writing and as a method of thinking with texts. Translators Corina Gepner (2019), Noémie Grunenwald (2021), Kate Briggs (2017), Polly Barton (2021), Ayesha Manazir Siddiqi (2022) and Diane Meur (2019), to name a few, have experimented with translation and autobiography to think and reflect on their literary translation practice in ways that mix both the critical and the poetic, mapping their practices experientially, as well as theoretically, in a way which both explores and questions the rules of engagement of translation. The authors just cited stand out for their intellectual exploration of translation as a craft, focusing on the thinking processes and embodied textual engagements with texts as a form of deeply situated critical theory which closely resembles what Lauren Fournier and others have recently defined as 'autotheory', a term which 'refers to the integration of theory and philosophy with autobiography, the body, and other so-called personal and explicitly subjective modes' (Fournier 2021: 7). They represent a form of autobiographical writing on, or about, translation practice which can both be mapped on the memoir form and deviate from it in so far as, borrowing the words of Maggie Nelson, they 'exceed the boundaries of the "personal"' to reach an exploratory and experimental theoretical practice (Nelson and McCrary 2015). In the next parts of this section, I will analyse the ways in which the autotheoretical translation memoir can be characterised by a process of unlearning disciplinary boundaries and forms in order to explore the embodied, tactile experience of translation practice. To think of theory as tactile, as rooted in practice and as embodied might seem contradictory, but it is a productive tension I will insist on by reading Barthes in conjunction with these works. Through this gesture, my aim is to weaken the boundaries between practice and theory in translation studies, and to advocate for a form of theory open to experimentation and critical engagement through creative-critical forms of autotheoretical reflection. A form of theory which, by softening the divisions between the object and the subject, practice (hand) and intellectual (head) in translation theory, has the potential to open translation studies to a wider field of inquiry and practice-based methods of research.

On Tact and Theory

Autotheory is a form of writing pioneered by writers such as Gloria Evangelina Anzaldúa (1987) in the 1980s and popularised, more recently, by Paul Preciado (2008) and Maggie Nelson (2009, 2015) to define a form of creative non-fiction distinct from the memoir insofar as it problematises the self in theorising. These works can be characterised as efforts to rethink theory from marginalised, racialised and queer bodies' perspectives and to revisit and deconstruct theoretical and political concepts of self from the heterogeneity of the body's experiential standpoint. As articulated by Lauren Fournier, autotheoretical works question the impersonality of theoretical production: 'Who can write or make work in ways that are understood as theory? The autotheoretical impulse, tied up as it is with intersectional feminist histories of bridging theory and practice, art and life, is entwined in these questions' (Fournier 2021: 48). They also challenge, in the case of Gloria Anzaldúa (1987), dominant linguistic narratives and monolingual paradigms of the self as a continuation of Western colonial logic, exposing how grand-narratives and theories of the self have touched and impacted the subjects they are idealising or abstracting.[1] In these works, theory itself becomes beholden to the objects and subjects traditionally scrutinised in academic contexts.

Ayesha Manazir Siddiqi's essay 'Preserving the Tender Things' is an autotheoretical exploration of her life and work as a translator. Her work challenges the conception of the translator as 'intermediary between the West and her local culture, and how this role of intermediary can in fact be very much a part of the colonial project' (Siddiqi 2022: 83). Opening her writing with a citation from Anzaldúa: 'I will have my serpent's tongue – my woman's voice, my sexual voice, my poets voice', she defines her work as 'a prayer for the tender things, those that become lost, damaged, or forgotten when a dominant language overtakes one less powerful' (Anzaldúa 1987: 23; Siddiqi 2022: 83). Published as part of a collection of personal reflections, interviews and essays entitled *Violent Phenomena* (2022) aiming to challenge forms of epistemic colonialism assumed in translation, Siddiqi structures her writing in two columns. Adopting the form of the memoir on the left, she reflects on hers and her family's personal relationship with Urdu and maps her personal trajectory

---

[1] For an illuminating reflection on the relationship between theory and touch, see Sarah Jackson, *Tactile Poetics: Touch and Contemporary Writing* (2015).

towards translation as a violent figuration of her linguistic and cultural experience. On the right, Siddiqi generally adopts a more academic tone to comment on her autobiographical writing in a manner which, at times, seems to create a critical distance between the reader and Siddiqi's personal narrative. The use of columns, as her presentation of this work as a 'personalised and semi-fictional "case study"', highlights the provisional division between the two forms of writing as a convention which her life exceeds, as the crossing of the line separating the two texts often demonstrates: 'How arbitrary all these borders are. They dissolve the moment you come in for a better look' (Siddiqi 2022: 83). Constantly inviting the reader to cross and swerve between the personal and the critical, Siddiqi reads the division between memoir and essay as an epistemological structuring which reinforces the ubiquity and neutrality of the colonial gaze:

What are these columns, by the way, meant to divide? Is it . . .	
Personal	Impersonal
Biography	Academic
Body	Mind?
How arbitrary all these borders are. They dissolve	the moment you come in closer for a better look
	(Siddiqi 2022: 89)

In her writing, Siddiqi questions not only the neutrality of the academic discourse on translation but the role assigned to translators when they are abstracted by academic discourse into the role of cultural mediators rather than cultural actors. Weakening the omniscience of the traditional critical gaze allows Siddiqi to trace a more detailed and rigorous account of translators' contextual engagement with culture, and to repair the violent mis-readings performed, at times, by the act of translating Urdu into the coloniser's language by writing back from the position of the translated as well as the translator.

Rather than theorising from the epistemological purview of an assumed objectivity, autotheoretical works often problematise the dichotomy between creativity and criticism by instigating reflections which stay close to the affective and sensorial details of experience, claiming them as legitimate knowledge worthy of investigation. Noting autotheory's effort to stay close to affective truths, Kris Pint and Maria Gill Ulldesmollins, for example, have highlighted the importance of Barthes in this 'third form of writing': 'While it might be a stretch to declare a direct lineage between all autotheory and Barthes, his work irrefutably opens possibilities for this third from. It is not surprising, then, that Barthes is often explicitly mentioned as an inspiration (Healy; Davey and

Nelson; Sayers)' (Pint and Gill Ulldesmollins 2020: 118). Similarly to Barthes in his later works[2] especially, autotheoretical works challenge the neutrality of the critical 'I' which judges translations on the grounds of invisibility and transparency, challenging the position of authority of theory over practice by confronting this distinction with translators' social existence and affects.

Echoing contemporary autotheory's interest in the forms of creative-critical practice inaugurated by Barthes, *This Little Art* (2017) explores Kate Briggs' approaches translating Barthes' works, and translation practice in general, as a critical gesture. *This Little Art* is an exercise in thinking *in* translation: of rewriting translation as a form of criticism and of rewriting criticism as a form of thinking. Like Barthes' works itself, it offers a writerly bridge between writing practice and theory by shining a light on the material and sensorial dimension of translation as a form of thinking. Briggs' *This Little Art*, then, is, more than a translation commentary, a continuation of the work of translation which Briggs undertook in her translation of Barthes from French into English. It adopts a model of practice-based criticism through translation which Briggs has stated could not have taken place in a more traditional academic form. Here, she recalls her feelings of not having done justice to the relationship between André Gide and Dorothy Bussy in an academic article she wrote prior to *This Little Art*:

> [W]hen I finished that article . . . I remember feeling like I'd killed it, this story I was trying to re-tell. I'd killed it by trying to make it do or stand in for something else. I was trying to use it as an example as a way of saying something broader about translation in general even though the basic argument of the article was to say: look how complicated it is to talk about translation in general, when this correspondence shows us that each translation-relation is each time so singular and so specific. (Briggs and LaRue 2017)

Particularly central to Briggs' argument in adopting a more subjective approach to writing about translation is Barthes' term 'délicatesse', which was translated into 'tact' by Rosalind Krauss and Denis Hollier's translation of *Le Neutre/The Neutral* (2002/2005). In Briggs' text, tact intimates a rereading of criticism from the point of view of translation as a manipulation and rewriting of texts: a tactile form of writing and thinking which adapts and changes in relation to its object.

'Délicatesse', a term Barthes explores in *The Preparation to the Novel* (2003/ 2011, translated by Kate Briggs) and *The Neutral* (2002/2005), is central to both her reflection on translation and her approach to translation criticism. For

---

[2] I am thinking of *La Chambre claire* (1980) and *Fragments d'un discours amoureux* (1977a) and *Roland Barthes par Roland Barthes* (1975) and *Journal de deuil* (1977b) especially.

Barthes, tact teaches us that to name is to touch others with language: 'Never separate a behavior from the account the subject gives of it, for the word penetrates the act throughout' (Barthes 2005: 58). To speak, to theorise, if we pursue this line of thinking, is thus always a form of touching that or who is being described in a way that could affect and possibly harm them. While the practice of criticism usually operates on the clear distinction between the subject and the object of criticism, Barthes reminds us on the contrary that there can be no theorisation without touch – in other words, that to theorise is to put into practice a certain form and ethic of relation. His subjective method of writing, then, is also a method of critical care which acknowledges the power of language to touch and affect whatever and whomever is described in it.

Barthes' definition of tact presents writing as a relational and haptic activity, as proceeding from a place of entanglement between language and matter which translators, as writers entrusted with the words of others, are all too aware of. While, far from new materialist concerns with scientific discourse, Barthes' and Briggs' approach to language, and therefore translation, echo, to some extent, new materialist critiques of scientific objectivity. Karen Barad explains: '[The relation of the social and the scientific] is not a static relationality but a doing – the enactment of boundaries – that always entails constitutive exclusions and therefore requisite questions of accountability' (Barad 2007: 803). Similarly, Briggs' reframing of translation as a making and a doing with words allows her to explore the critical responsibility of recreating forms in translation. Likewise, Siddiqi's 'Prayer for the Tender Things' can be read in light of Barthes as a challenge to the unassumed violence of the right to epistemic access in translation practice. In her exploration of care in and as translation, Siddiqi counters an imperialist logic of contact at all costs with an ethic of tact and attention, creating a text which can neither be caught nor readily consumed.

Adopting Krauss and Hollier's translation of 'délicatesse' as 'tact' in English allows Briggs to trouble the distinction between translation criticism and translation practice in her memoir (Briggs 2017: 325). Based on her reading of Barthes, Briggs defines tact as 'the art of not treating all things in the same way. Of treating *what appears to be the same* as though different' (Briggs 2017: 327). Although 'general working definitions' of translation are not wrong, she argues, they also impede our understanding of what translation can do in different contexts by not being attentive enough to the differences between differences:

> What Barthes identifies as a breach of tact is the feeling of being reduced to
> a category that is too big. A great big class of actors and of activity, a kind of
> catch-all box. One that holds us all – translation is more or less translation,

and translators are more or less translators, everywhere – but for just that reason cannot begin to attend to our different motivations, our specific desires, our peculiar joys and distresses. (Briggs 2017: 320)

Her experimental memoir practice can be read as a critical engagement to weaken strong definitions of translation in favour of the form of 'douceur' (which Briggs in this context translates into 'sweetness', but which can also mean 'softness') of approach which Barthes argues can help us apprehend the world with more tact (Briggs 2017: 324). It is in this sense that the 'little' in the title *This Little Art* is apprehended in Briggs' work: 'to the extent that I can hear it – that I can make it – speak of an art of attending to all the small differences' (Briggs 2017: 328). Translation can, in this context, be redefined, beyond its interlinguistic dimension, as a way of approaching a subject or task with the attentiveness it requires: one which demands a temporary weakening of theory for the sake of attention. A form of reading which requires, like translation, that the approach itself be adaptive and unique, created and creative. Weakening the universal power of theoretical claims, in this context, allows for a more adaptive and materially informed reading of translation practice.

Formal Digression

Self and theoretical digression play a central role in the processes of theorisation proper to the translation memoir as autotheory. A digression is etymologically, 'a going away', a 'departing' but also a deviation from what are normally subject and object positions in theorisation.[3] For Kathleen Stewart, weak theory is 'theory that comes unstuck from its own line of thought to follow the objects it encounters, or be undone by its attention to things that don't just add up but take life of their own as problems for thoughts' (Stewart 2008: 72). Digressing is, thus, a poetic strategy with a theoretical edge which allows autotheoretical translation memoirs to stay with the theoretical-affective 'troubles' of translating (Haraway 2016).

In the translation memoir as autotheory, digression takes place not only narratively but formally, allowing a growing variety of media and writing genres to meet in the creative testimonial accounts of translational practice. Such use of digression as a creative-critical strategy is evident, for example, in Siddiqi's essay-memoir, in which a narrative voice invites us to re-imagine her essay in the shape of a snake: 'I want to end with a secret, if that's ok. Come closer, and please, promise this remains between you and me, ok? Ok. Well, this essay is also like a snake. It shed its skin many times before reaching you'

---

[3] www.collinsdictionary.com/dictionary/english/digress.

(Siddiqi 2022: 101). In this epilogue that opens up the text to multiple reading methods more than it closes it, Siddiqi invites us to re-imagine writing as a provisional and temporary form. Like a snake shedding its skin, her auto-theoretical text is a performative space in which different translatorial voices and selves have been assumed and abandoned. Translation memoirs such as Siddiqi's, then, give us a point of entry in which to theorise 'translatorial practice' both as literary performance and as social practice.

Unlike traditional memoirs, autotheoretical translation memoirs consider the subject of writing not as a singular point of reference but as a form to rewrite, translate and remediate through the practice of translation. In *Entre les Rives* (*Between Shores*, my translation, 2019), for example, Diane Meur, a writer and translator of German fiction into French, mixes different writing genres to explore her translational practice. This generic hybridity operates not only as a tool to explore the subject of translation through different angles but to translate her experiences as a translator in different forms and media. Memoir, interview, self-translation, comparative translation commentary and essay all appear to be different ways of 'translating' and examining her work as a translator from different angles. In so doing, Meur playfully translates her personal account of translating into different genres while bringing our attention to the performative, and therefore translational, gesture inherent in all forms of memoir writing.

Throughout the text, the 'I' of the memoir appears to be translated into different generic forms, stressing the translator's co-construction in writing. Her first section opens on a personal account of her incessant attempts to translate a poem by Hofmannsthal, recounting the childhood memory which made her realise she wanted to become a writer. While some passages focus exclusively on her search for the right translation, others try to theorise Meur's thinking on the difficulty of translating certain literary genres, such as the diary:

> This diary's specific problem: the almost spoken sentences with its lose syntax and literal meanings that remain rather vague, even if we understand very well the ideas behind it. To translate these types of sentences, I have to create a distance between myself and the words and to let the spoken effect of the sentence act on me. (Meur 2019: 45, my translation)

Meur's playful use of literary genres theorises the translator's position as a performer, a performance she continues to enact in the first-person account of her work as a translator. Her performative drifting between genres is one which, in the words of Della Pollock, allows her to '[enfold] in writing the "I" modernity and postmodernity generally cut up and cut out: the passionate, excessive, errant, collective, and often exuberantly irregular "I" excluded by the systematic reproduction of sameness' (Pollock 1998: 24). The multiple exposure strategy used by Meur allows her to adopt a diffracted, as opposed to a reflexive approach, to her practice: rather than reifying and reinforcing her subjectivity as a writer-translator, she is using different subject positions in the text as a research method to analyse her translational practice and delimit her responsibilities and agency as a translator.

In a passage where she reflects on her relationship with an author whose work she has translated, for example, Meur relates her experience of negotiating her translational choices. Up until then, she reflects, she had always followed the wishes of the author when they had decided to erase a word or change part of the text in the translation. A letter criticising her translation changed her opinion on the matter: 'after all, I am the one signing the translation. As such, I must be responsible for my choices'. Meur follows with an attempt to theorise her position in relation to authors' authority over translators more broadly: 'All this made me think, and I found the beginnings of a theory. I have to make a distinction between the intention of the author and their will' (Meur 2019: 49, my translation). Further theorising her position allows Meur to explore her own ethical relation to the text in a way which reconciles her responsibilities as a translator with her duty towards the author – but it also reveals something of the power relations at play within translational norms. Who will bear responsibility if the translation is badly received as a result of the author's choices? A translation in her name but which did not belong to her would be a way of abdicating her own critical agency as a translator.

Loosening her theoretical approach to traditional autobiography as an instrument for maintaining distinct subject positions allows her to trace a more granular analysis of the fleeting moments of reflection on her craft, making it possible for her to stay close to the affective truths of her experience. It allows her to research, analyse and speculate about her own relation to translation somatically, to borrow Robinson's term, from the embodied perspective of its practice but also in relation to wider ethical concerns tied in with the act of translation as a socially situated practice (Robinson 1991).

Adopting a principle of tact in her writing, Briggs' herself follows a translation criticism model which is provisional and experimental rather than ontologising. *This Little Art* is full of passages where, instead of a lofty perspective on her subject, the 'I' of writing backtracks, corrects herself, returns and changes her opinion as she writes. Like a translator who performs others' voices, the 'I' speaking and thinking is often seen adorning different clothes, different voices until it declares that it has found one that fits. Her performative approach to writing, Briggs explains, redefines the essay from the perspective of translation as an essayistic practice. Analysing her attempts, in *This Little Art*, to convey her experience of translating Barthes as a matter of 'establishing Barthes's "I" and then slowly disinvesting him of this "I" and investing myself in that speaking or writing position', she explains:

> I wanted to explore the complication of all of this: what it is to take on someone else's phrasing, the thinking formulated in sentences written by someone else, and pushing it through your own body. That's where the dance and the aerobics come in – the idea that these are your moves that I see you make, Instructor. But now I'm doing them. Now I'm taking them on, and testing what happens when *I* try them. . . . This seems to me a way of getting at the experimentalism I think is inherent in every act of translation: what it is to re-do something ourselves, to re-make some gesture, re-write some sentence, without knowing – without having any real way of knowing in advance – what will happen when we do. (Briggs and LaRue 2017)

In *This Little Art*, then, Briggs portrays translation as an exercise in tact that is alive to translation as a form of physical embodiment of someone else's writing practice: one with the responsibility that comes with the power of touching the cultures, subjects and voices it performs. To translate this experience to the reader, Briggs eschews the lofty and linear discourse of rational expertise on translation to adopt a more draft-like, essay-like form of writing modelled on translation practice. An essay in the form of a translation draft of her experience of translating Barthes and the works of translating: one in which she tries on (from the French 'essayer'), experiments with language in order to translate her experience of translating Barthes. As such, her work is also a way of rethinking the memoir, of rewriting it, from the perspective of translation as an experiment in translating the other into one's own language, in being occupied and in occupying someone else's language: an experiment, in other words, in being *with* another by sharing a space of enunciation. An experiment in what Barthes would call 'living together' (Barthes 2002/2013).

Translation as Feminist Practice

Like all autotheoretical works, translations which mix autobiography and creative-critical translation practice run the risk of being labelled egotistical. Autotheoretical works by feminist writers for example have long been treated with suspicion under the pretext of being too self-centred. As Fournier notes, these charges have their roots in feminist writing practices:

> One of the most noticeable ways in which the autotheoretical turn is tied to histories of feminist practice is the simple fact that feminist artists continually face the charge of narcissim when they incorporate themselves in direct ways into their work (and feminists themselves are not immune from launching

> such critiques). One of the reasons why work by women and artists of color is particularly vulnerable to charges of narcissism is that women and racialized people have been historically overdetermined by their bodies – in contrast, always, to the supposedly neutral standard of the white, cisgender man. (Fournier 2021: 43)

For Fournier, autotheory challenges the Cartesian dualism at the root of this charge by questioning the apparent impersonality of criticism. Although a seemingly objective description of translation studies as an area of knowledge, Holmes' separation of practice and theory, for example, reinforces a hierarchy between traditionally gendered roles in translation as well as a particular model of epistemological production. What is presented as an objective definition of a field of knowledge or practice naturalises a distinction between translation practice and translation theory which is, in reality, historically and culturally contingent on Western epistemology. Grunenwald's *Sur les bouts de la langue: Traduire en féministe/s* (2021), as we shall see, presents translation in a way which makes apparent this unexamined network of power relations, giving us to see translation practice as a feminist method in self-emancipation and trans-formation which in turn can serve as a tool of collective transformation.

In this first-person account of her translation practice, Grunenwald explores the polyphonic transformation of her voice through translation as a form of self-experimentation which reaches beyond the personal to the political. For her, translation is a way of thinking with others she translates, and of actively hybridising herself in the process:

> My writing is not the same before or after a translation. It is true that with time, the imprints of a translation weaken. But perhaps they are only less noticeable, diluted as they are in the multiplication of influences. I am not looking for a form of pure creation but a pertinent assemblage of inspirations. The exploration of an intertext. I dream of making a book out of cut and pasted citations following one another. . . . This is what I conceive to be text work, whether this be in the form of translation, editing or writing: a work that is profoundly collective. (Grunenwald 2021: 56, my translation)

Here, Grunenwald re-imagines translation not only as a method of re-inventing her own voice but of unlearning the contours of traditional writing method and its modes of subjectivisation. Her method of translation is also a method of self-intervention, a way of engineering different subject positions from the perspec-tive of translation by re-imagining writing, often thought of as a solitary practice, into a collective practice: 'My translations fill me up. When I write, I reproduce them in content and form. I am filled with the references of the women authors I translate' (Grunenwald 2021: 55). This description of transla-tion practice as (ful)filment is reminiscent of Bernard Stiegler's concept of transindividuation, where 'both the "I" and the "We" are transformed through one another'. For Stiegler, transindividuation, rather than the individuals, forms 'the basis for all social transformation' but also creativity (Rogoff and Stiegler 2010: 1). According to Stiegler, interiorising

> social circuits within cerebral circuits is what permits the constitution of transindividuation processes. Signification is itself the material of what Winnicott calls creativity, which echoes what Canguilhem calls normativity. And creativity is what produces meaning from significations shared by those who co-individuate themselves through a process of transindividuation. (Stiegler 2013: 5)

Similarly, throughout her memoir, Grunenwald acknowledges the work and influence of others in constructing her vision of feminism as a form of collective construction of the term through, and in, translation. But this creative approach to feminism is not one done in spite of, but because of its collective and transindividual dimension.

Similarly, in *This Little Art*, Briggs often acknowledges, invites even, the reader to take part in the intimacy of the book's collaborative method of criticism and translation: 'I imagine that for you, too, there must be a sentence. A paragraph. Or a longer part of someone else's work that you feel you know well' (Briggs 2017: 201). Through Briggs' reflection on translation as a performative practice, translation is represented as a pleasure that can be shared: a way of experiencing a text, of embodying other voices by rewriting them in different languages. But this share-taking of the pleasure of reading a text also raises important questions regarding text ownership. Whose text is a translation? It is also possible to read Briggs and Grunenwald's autotheoretical works as a rewriting of translation in light of such questions of ownership and practice: an experiential but also creative-critical translation of translation practice. A way of rewriting translation criticism which will transform how we see and think about translation.

Echoing Brigg's exploration of ownership and voice in translation, Grunenwald's autotheoretical memoir not only hybridises writing formally and vocally, but poly-authorially too, in a way which seeks to acknowledge her own writing as a co-laboured process. Towards the end of the book, Grunenwald defines feminist translation as a way of loving other women: 'Not a fetish-love but a composite-love', she explains. 'Not an isolating love but a weaving love' (Grunenwald 2021: 139, my translation). The weaving and composite nature of her affective engagement is also reproduced in her performative redefinition of the translation memoir, and therefore of autobiography, as a collective process. In a passage where she remembers finding three sewing kits in her grand-mother's apartment following her death, Grunenwald uses them to weave three important women in her writing, illustrating them with photographs in a way that is both moving and politically intentional (Figure 2).

Grunenwald's re-embodiment of intellectual memory through the portraits of women from her family that she weaves into the text is also a way of crossing class and gender divisions in her book: a way of opening the door to silent workers and helpers without whom she would not have been able to translate and write. In what Sedgwick would call a 'reparative' gesture, Grunenwald queers the form of the memoir, stretches its textual fabric so it may accommodate portraits of the invisible women who have sustained her, or whose life stories, such as her aunt's suicide, have accompanied her in her own journey into feminist and queer theory (Grunenwald 2021: 148–50). Forcing open the book as an institution and as a form of symbolic capital, Grunenwald seems to metaphorically hang the portraits of her late family members to repair and mend the division between manual and intellectual labour inherited from notions of class and gender distinctions.

Both Briggs and Grunenwald invite us to re-consider authorship and translation from a broader material and social perspective. The autobiographical dimension of hers and Briggs' texts are, far from a narcissistic exercise, a way of remapping the human relations at work in creation beyond more rigid and gendered separations between translation practice and translation theory.

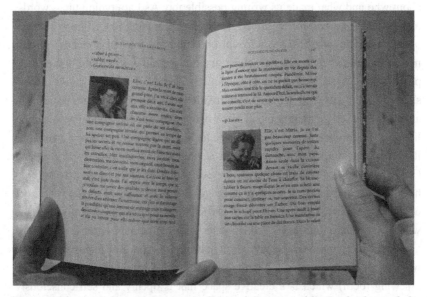

Figure 2 Photo of pages 116 and 117 of Noémi Grunenwald's *Sur les bouts de la langue: Traduire en féministe/s* (2021)

Adopting a mobile and flexible subject position by using translation as a form of self-experimentation allows them to evade captivity from dominant forms of thinking. Abandoning the traditional facelessness of translation theory and literary criticism allows them to examine the relationship between translation practice and the material world from an embodied, experiential perspective. It is also a way of asking: in the historicised and contextualised map of translation as a field, who does the practice, and who does the thinking?

This re-imagining of translation in both Briggs' and Grunenwald's autobiographical practices are thus not only self-transformative for the translators but capable of theorising writing beyond the privatisation of labour encapsulated by a disembodied notion of authorship. The reworlding of the text through the medium of another time, place, language and relation that is the work of translation is therefore also, when translated into autotheoretical form, a work of re-embodiment and a material re-inscription of the spectral work of translation. As an authorial remainder of the translated text, the autotheoretical translation memoir thus can be seen to act as a reinvestment of the text into material realities normally pushed to the paratextual peripheries of the book as an institution, when it is not altogether invisible. The translation memoir as autotheory is thus a re-embodiment of the text, but also, as we have seen, of translation practice as a field of research and method of becoming.

Before I conclude, I will give myself permission to engage in an autotheoretical digression of my own: in the context of working on this Section, I have thought about who and what made its writing possible too. As I am typing these words, my mother is waiting for me in the next room, preparing food. I have hurt my back, and she has come over to help with childcare. Her kitchen labour as a gift for my writing time. My mother's help is just one example of writing being made possible by material propping and collective sustenance. If authorship is ownership by way of one's own labour, the translation memoir as autotheory is, far from an exercise in self-aggrandisement, a way of approaching the labour of translation literature in a broader sense. Because nothing is ever simply 'authored', wouldn't it be better to think of texts as being 'laboured' and indeed, as Briggs and Grunenwald show us 'co-laboured', or co-crafted, by more than one helping hand? After all, the making of texts, as Briggs demonstrates, is extended in the act of reading and translating as forms of participation, remaking a text into a place where one meets, discusses, collaborates and sometimes argues. A text as a participative endeavour, a relational matrix, an open and inclusive map of work: what comes to my mind in the shape of the word 'ouvroir' (a workroom, a sewing room) which is a creative space that is openly and self-consciously collaborative and co-creative. A form of writing which acknowledges its material entanglements and co-dependence on a wide network of actors and factors.

Conclusion

Autotheoretical translation memoirs, then, subvert the myth that translation theory and practice exist on different planes, that translation theory can be 'applied' and 'reach' translation practice without remediation – in short, that doing translation theory is akin to injecting some thinking into what is wrongly thought of as 'the simple act of linguistic reproduction' that is thought to be translation. While the autotheoretical translation memoir does this, like all memoirs, partly from the purview of 'hindsight', it is also a journey, like all autotheoretical works, in self-transformation and therefore self-translation. One in which a relation is created anew with each critical encounter, which is to say one in which, in the manner of translation, there can be no theory, no form of representation, without touch and responsibility. A weaker theory, which solicits creativity as a method of critical adaptability.

Rather than portraying translation as a form of hermeneutic knowledge, a way of close-reading texts which might be key to understanding their intrinsic nature, the autotheoretical translation memoir thus offers a practice-based model of translation criticism as well as a model of creative-critical practice. The translation memoir, in other words, is a rethinking of theory from the point of view of translation and the translator in 'flesh' and 'blood' (Pym 2014: 4), one which posits the right to approach theory with critical care and attention to small details which might escape grand-narratives of theoretical classification. While it is a form which does engage at times with a traditional hermeneutic of suspicion, it does not apply it systematically – making space, instead, for moments of detachment from existing paradigms of translation and (re)attachment to others, at times adding voice and depth to their objects of translation in the process. Formally, we may apprehend the autotheoretical translation memoir as a post-critical exercise in the sense that it builds, as Rita Felski puts it, 'an ampler and more diverse range of theoretical vocabularies' (Felski 2015: 181). As a form of autotheory inspired by the interstitial and experimental relationship between translator and translation, autotheoretical translation memoirs adopt a creative and formally innovative approach to both translation theory and to methods of self-theorisation, one modelled on translation as a form of relational configuration and transindividuation.

2 Performative Translations

On a recent second trip to Rome, I had the opportunity to look at many paintings by Caravaggio in various museums and churches across the city. One of them was a representation of Bacchus (Figure 3).

Figure 3 Michelangelo Merisi, known as Caravaggio, *Bacchus*, 1598 c., oil on canvas, 95 x 85 cm

Normally represented as an old man with a beard or as an idealised youth, Caravaggio chooses instead to represent Bacchus as a young man in disguise. The originality of the painting lies precisely in the distance between the myth as it is traditionally represented and the modern setting depicted by Caravaggio. What I see is not simply a reproduction of Bacchus idealised either as an old or a young deity, but a depiction of a Bacchus 'dress up'. A camp Bacchus, revelling and revealing forms of artifice and exaggeration which such pictorial reproductions normally tone down (Sontag 1981: 275). What gives it all away? Is it the flush on his cheeks or the air of boredom on his face which could signal the discomfort of a prolonged pose? Is it the nonchalant way he is reclining, or the extravagant swathes of vine leaves and grapes adorning him? Or this detail: the aged and brown cushion with a blue stripe under the hastily arranged white robe of the subject. In an idealised representation of Bacchus, all of these elements would have been smoothed and edited out of the final painting; but not in Caravaggio's works. Like all paintings of Bacchus, Caravaggio's work is about excess. However, the excess we see no longer points solely to Bacchus as a subject matter, but to the accumulated details of historical repetition, and the lavish rehearsal of its reproductions. What speaks in this painting is not simply the myth of Bacchus, but the very practice of repeating it which is signed and performed, as it were, in the visibility of the present of posing and painting as Bacchus. It is as if Caravaggio were saying: 'here you are, I give you not Bacchus himself, but *another one*, one more representation, with some twists you will recognise'. In this playful reflection of painting and posing as 'Bacchus', a liminal space of exploration between creativity and criticism is intimated, allowing Caravaggio to explore 'the unstable improvisations within our deep cultural performances; [exposing] the fissures, ruptures, and revisions that have settled into continuous re-enactement' (Diamond 1996: 2). As viewers of the painting, we are interpellated, in the Althusserian sense of the term, to partake not in the reconstruction of the myth, but in the critical interrogation of both cultural and gender norms which are reproduced within it.

In this Section, I will turn my attention to translations which, instead of striving to repeat originals by performing hegemonic norms of faithfulness, have explored the performative dimension of translation through a creative-critical rewriting of translation norms. I will call such translations 'performative translations' and, in the first half of this Section, I will explain what I mean by this term through my analysis of Charles Bernstein, Erin Mouré and Karoline Bergvall's works. Just as Della Pollock argued that writing itself can be performative by identifying 'the need to make writing speak *as* writing' (Pollock 1998: 76), I will argue that translation, too, has the ability to perform its own translatedness by acting out the transformative encounters of the source text with another language, culture and temporality. What happens when translations signify and display themselves as art? What happens, in other words, when translation norms become performative subjects in a translation? In the second half of this Section, I will focus on how Anne Carson's translation of Sappho's texts have performed their own interpretation of feminine desire through the medium of translation. My aim is to show that Carson's translation intervenes in traditionally masculine representations of Sappho in translation and in painting which have turned Sappho into an object, rather than the subject, of desire by displacing her authorial agency in the text. Carson, as we shall see, translates Sappho's authorial voice by materialising it reflexively in translation, giving feminine desire a body and agency in translation itself.

Performing Translation as Creative-Critical Practice

In the sense given to the term by J. L. Austin (1955/1962), a performative utterance is an utterance that is part of a doing: a declaration, such as 'you are now husband and wife', which in itself has the power to enact or 'perform' the union. As Theo Hermans aptly remarked in *The Conference of Tongues*, all translations are to some extent performative in the sense that Austin understood the term: what we call translation as opposed to an original work is in part reliant on the paratextual framing of translations which sign or declare translations to be translations (Hermans 2007). Prefaces to translations, he points out, are often such ways of framing a text as a translation to the reader. 'In this way', Hermans remarks, 'a translator's preface prevents an uninhibited reading of the translation because its echo can still be heard while the performance is under way' (Hermans 2007: 42–3). In this sense, as Hermans demonstrates, for a translation to be a translation, it needs to be interpellated as one through paratextual means: the paratext is therefore a way to structure our reading into separating translation from originals.

What happens when, similarly to Carravagio's *Bacchus*, a translation is not only recognised as a translation a posteriori, but when it performs its own translatedness? What happens when translations raise the performance of translation to the reader's consciousness? Harnessing recent analysis exploring the relationship between translation and performativity (Hermans 2007; Bermann 2014; Kadiu 2019; Pacheco Aguilar and Guénette 2021), my focus will extend to translations which have performed themselves as an artistic practice, thereby visibilising translation as an artistic and literary subject in its own right. By performing themselves or by being performed, performative translations force us to pay attention to the artfulness of translation, foregrounding translation not only as a form of reproduction, but as a potential field of creative-critical intervention.

What forms of critical interventions might performative translations make possible? Central to the argument I will be making is the well-established idea that translation is a norm-governed activity (Toury 1995; Schäffner 1999). Indeed, as well as reproducing texts, translations also reproduce norms which 'carry within them the values shared by a community' (Schäffner 1999: 1). Thus, as well as harmonising translation practice, translation norms also reinforce the social values from which they spring. As Hermans explains: 'norms and conventions contribute to the stability of interpersonal relations, and hence of groups, communities and societies, by reducing contingency, unpredictability, and the uncertainty which springs from our inability to control time or to predict the actions of fellow human beings' (Hermans 1996: 26).

In the sense that translations reproduce norms as well as texts, translations also take part in what Bourdieu called cultural and social reproduction (Bourdieu 1973). For translation norms, like any other form of value-driven social practice, can interpellate readers into pre-existing categories, assumptions and cartographies of difference. Performative translations, I propose, can prompt readers to think about the nature of what is reproduced through translation norms by bringing attention to them. They are an attempt to investigate and therefore theorise translation as a poetic practice and conceptual performance in its own right.

Performing and making visible translations as art can indeed raise many questions as to the nature of translation as a form of reproduction. Charles Bernstein's 'A Test of Poetry' in *Chain 10* (2003) and its translations into Brazillian Portuguese, Finnish, Spanish and French by De Campo, Lehto, Livon Grosman and Traduction Collective a Royaumont are a case in point. The poem, based on a letter written by the Chinese scholar and translator Ziquing Zhang to Bernstein while he attempted to translate his works, is a sequence of questions to the author about the meaning of certain expressions in his poems. Together with its translations, it constitutes a kind of experimental translation laboratory, what I am tempted to call an experimental 'translation zone' beyond the geopolitical sense given to it by Emily Apter (2006): a form of experimental translation laboratory revolving around translation practice. Here is the first stanza of the poem in English:

> What do you mean by *rashes of ash*? Is industry
> systematic work, assiduous activity, or ownership
> of factories? Is *ripple* agitate lightly? Are
> we tossed in tune when we write poems? And
> what or *who emboss with gloss insignias of air*?
> *(Bernstein 2003: 20)*

'A Test of Poetry' can be read as a found poem which explores the testing or 'trials' (to use Berman's terminology in Venuti's translation (Berman 2021)) of translation on the original and its language. But it also constitutes, to the extent that this form of questioning is latent to all translational processes and constitutes an attempt to understand the poem, a translation of Bernstein's poem in its own right. Here, both translation and translation commentary are inseparable: the translator's questions to Bernstein show that translation is always a theorisation and a questioning that demands creative solutions. What Bernstein's poem highlights, then, is that translation is at once an interpretive and a creative gesture: but rather than being something that can only be solved by the author as the source of meaning, this questioning of the text can only ever be solved by rewriting, translating and transforming the text. In other words, by what Barbara Godard would call 'a transformance': a repetition that is also a transformation (Godard 1991). Bernstein's poem, together with its translations, then, inaugurate a translation zone in which questions pertaining to the meaning of Bernstein's poem can only be answered by the translator rather than the author.

The Chinese translator's search for equivalence and meaning in translating Bernstein's poems unfolds into a semantic crisis in the poem. The questions, although intended to search for linguistic equivalence, seem to raise semantic ambivalence in the English language instead, prompting the translator to translate the poem into English to focus its meaning. While the poem in English cannot and does not answer the questions, the translations into other languages seem, at least in part, to propose a solution to them for the translator by translating 'rashes of ash' into 'urticaire de cendre', or 'ripple' into 'onduler', for example:

> Que veux tu dire par *urticaire de cendre* ? Est-ce qu'*industrie*
> Désigne le travail systématique, l'activité assidue ou la propriété
> D'usines ? *Onduler*, est-ce remuer légèrement ? Est-on
> Porté par le ton quand on écrit des poèmes ? Et
> Qui ou quoi *estampe avec les insignes brillants de l'air* ?
> *(Bernstein 2003: 35)*

The irony of translating these questions and the citations of the poem-to-be-translated they contain should not be lost on us: that any answer to these questions directly in English, even by Bernstein, would amount to a greater betrayal of the source poems' wonderful ambivalence than its translations into other languages. The lesson from this translation performance seems to be that poetry is not what is lost, but what is preserved and lives on in the translation of the source text into other languages, as Benjamin argues in 'The Translator's Task' (Benjamin 1923/2021). Unlike any other form of criticism or explanation of the source text in English, translations of the poem into other languages stay closer to its ambivalence by being able to perform it.

What a 'Test of Poetry' and its translations seem to test, of course, is the idea that poetry is that which cannot be translated. This translation philosophy is extended in the following statement made by Bernstein when asked to comment on Frost's famous apocrypha:

> I disagree with Robert Frost's often quoted remark that poetry "is lost . . . in translation." For me, poetry is always a kind of translation, transformation, transposition, and metamorphosis. There is nothing "outside" translation: no original poem or idea, nor one perfect translation. It's a matter of choosing among versions. Translation is a form of reading or interpreting or thinking with the poem. In that sense, there can be no experiencing the poem, even in your own language, without translating. Without translation the poem remains just a text, a document, a series of inert words. Poetry is what is found in translation. (Bernstein 2015)

By testing, in practice, theoretical assumptions made on behalf of translation and translators, Bernstein and his translators signify, in performance, what Barbara Godard called 'a turning, a making strange through a recontextualization that opens new networks of fields in which to situate a gesture, a body, a word' (Godard 1991: 11). Turning the question of the impossibility of interlinguistic equivalence on its head, and focusing the spotlight of equivalence on intralingual communication, Bernstein shows interlingual translations to be the most faithful reproductions of poetry's ambivalence, above and beyond any critical explanation of that text in the same language. What if, 'A Test of Poetry' asks us, conventional translation norms were based on an erroneous understanding of sameness and difference in language(s)?

By introducing 'a breach in social relations', Barbara Godard explains, 'performance works through a crisis, moving into the liminal, into the betwixt and between to furnish a critique of the crisis' (Godard 1991: 11). Performative translations operate similarly: introducing a breach where transparency and a translation's invisibility would be the norm, they make visible and work with the material realities of translation to transform our understanding of language and our linguistic presumptions about linguistic equivalence. What is enunciated in translation is no longer an imagined, idealised transaction between languages, but a zone of potentially far-reaching cultural transformation and critique. Re-contextualised beyond romantic assumptions about identity and differences, translation becomes, in the words of Judith Butler, 'the condition of a transformative encounter, a way of establishing alterity at the core of [normative] transmission' (cited in Butler 2012: 17; Bermann 2014: 295). Bernstein, De Campo, Lehto, Livon Grosman and Traduction Collective a Royaumont's performative translation zone thus rewrites our understanding of critique itself as the most able form of self-exploration of one's own culture, proposing translation as a practice-based critical engagement with poetry instead.

My aim now is not to present an exhaustive list of performative translation in all its forms but to give a selective overview of what appears to me to be some of its noticeable features and creative-critical potential based on the limited examples I have so far come across:

1. **The performative translation performs its trans-latedness.** It is not only, as Venuti describes, that performative translations render the translator visible in the translated text: more than making the presence of the translator visible in the text, the performative translation actively and self-consciously tries to stage translation writing as one reading or performance of a text among others. As such, performative translations are, similarly to Caravagio's *Bacchus*, conscious of their own 'belatedness'. But rather than seeing translation as a process between two points:

   The Original → The Translation

   The performative translation stages the cultural and linguistic conversations animating their translational relation with the source texts. Understood as provisional performance, performative translations create a chiasm between the referentiality assumed in the fiction of the source text and the present of translation. When translations are performative, time's presence is always diffracted by the temporality of translation, opening up the possibility of different temporal addresses within the text. The translation, in this context, performs its own 'lateness' by inscribing the present of translating in the fabric of the text. Exploring the temporality of translation in Anne Carson's *Antigonick*, for example, Ben Hjorth notes that: 'in Carson's translation, not only is Antigone fiercely self-conscious, moreover she seems to occupy a locutionary and performative position that traverses and problematizes chronological temporality itself'. By staging its own translatedness and there-fore 'belatedness', Carson's Antigone 'is one that brings the temporality of this practice into direct interrogation, in both its form and its content' (Hjorth 2014: 135). More than a mimesis, or a self-reflection of the same, performa-tive translations provide a way of cutting and intervening on the temporal iteration of difference which underpin translational conventions. By staging themselves as translations, performative translations become a zone capable of contesting and rethinking, through practice, how we connect, shape and involve others (audiences, participants, readers, citizens) through the perform-ance of translational repetition. In a way that is similarly relevant, as we shall see next, to Carson's translation of Sappho, Carson's *Antigonick* 'knit[s] the reception of *Antigone* into the play itself, letting us know that our only access to this play is through this present time, and yet showing that this time is still bound to that classical one' (Butler 2019: 382).

2. **The performative translation is citational.** Unlike other texts, translations do not usually cite or even acknowledge other translations. Instead, translations are usually called on to perform the original as an original, giving the impression to readers of translations that they have unmediated access to the source text. Performative translations, on the other hand, operate a critique of referentiality in translation practice by explicitly acknowledging or even citing past transla-tions, thereby blurring the boundary between citation and commentary, transla-tion and translation criticism. They foreground, in other words, the processual action of translation in the sense developed by Barbara Cassin as the 'intradui-sible'. In her chapbook *Elisa Sampedrín and the Paradox of Translation, or The Intranslatable*, Moure notes that in its version for the English *Dictionary of the Untranslatable*, 'intraduisible' is translated as the 'untranslatable', and Cassin's statement that the 'intraduisible' is 'ce qu'on ne cesse pas de (ne pas) traduire' becomes 'what one keeps on (not) translating' (Cassin 2004/2014: xvii). When translated by Burghard Baltrusch as the 'intranslatable' in English (Baltrusch 2018), Moure argues, the intranslatable becomes 'what one does not cease to (not) translate' (Cassin 2004: xvii; translated by Moure 2021: 20). Unlike the 'untranslatable', Moure notes that 'intranslatable', a term chosen by Baltrusch

based on the Brazilian Portuguese 'intradução', does not carry the same connotation of failure (Moure 2021: 18). According to Isabel Gómez's study of de Campos' coinage of 'intradução' in the 1970s, de Campos' 'intradução' 'rejects a norm of literary criticism where translation and literature both become invisible in favour of the self-sustaining discourse of criticism itself' (Gómez 2018: 381). Tracing a genealogy of 'intradução' in de Campos' writing, Gómez shows de Campos' use of the term to be 'flexible, shifting along with the larger game Campos plays with prefixes, negation, and repetition' (Gómez 2018: 381). Similarly to de Campos' use of the term, Moure's intranslation is an invitation for reader-writers to enter, alongside the translator, the process of translating. Moure further translates 'intranslation' as follows: The translator is the one whose task or duty is to (not) put an end to translation's own task, though they must – in the end – sign their name to one ebb of a flux that has not yet (ever) ceased (not) to take place, and may (not) not be "in progress," even though it be "published." (Moure 2021: 21).

This understanding and rewriting of translation as an unending 'flux' and cooperative process is put into practice by Moure in examples where she inscribes herself in the process of translation begun by others, either by re-inscribing a translated text in a different context or by interpreting it for her own practice. For Moure as for de Campos, translation is a thinking that is inseparable from a doing. Performing-explaining 'intranslation' by retranslating Richard Howard's translation of Roland Barthes, she writes:

> A readerly text is one I cannot re-produce (today I cannot write like Atwood); a writerly text is one I can read only if I utterly transform my reading regime. I now recognize a third text alongside the readerly and the writerly: let's call it the intranslatable. The intranslatable is the unreaderly text which catches fire, burns in the mouth, an instance continuously outside any likelihood, whose function – ardently assumed by its scripter – is to contest the mercantile constraints on what is written.
>
> *Roland Barthes by Roland Barthes*
> Richard Howard translation, altered by Ruin E. Rome
> (Moure and Pato 2014: 8)

Rather than retranslating Barthes' words from French, thereby writing *over* other past translations, Moure inscribes her translation in an intertextual relation with other translations. This intranslative gesture acknowledges the work of translators who came before her, interpellating and summoning into existence a community of Barthes 'interpreters' and 'readers' in other languages who have never ceased to 'intranslate' Barthes. To intranslate, then, is to step into this performative space of interpretation held open by translation as a performative practice.

The provisionality and openness to contestation of performative translations also manifests in Carolyn Bergvall's 'Via' (Bergvall 2003). In this textual and citational performance, Bergvall reproduces translated pieces of Dante Alighieri's *Divine Comedy*. In its version published in *Chain 10*, 'Via' reproduces forty-seven translations into English of Dante's opening lines of 'The Inferno'. She presents her work as follows: 'Translations into English of Dante's Inferno as archived by the British Library – Spring 2000 (700 years after the year fixed by Dante for the start of the journey)' (Bergvall 2003: 59). Numbered and ordered alphabetically, each of the reproduced translations invites a critical comparison of each stanza and the aesthetic experience of their repetition. In 'Via', Laura Goldstein explains, '"I" echoes through the historical time of literary scholarship as well as the real time of reading' (Godstein 2009). Using the page as a 'dramatic space', that is, by staging translation, Bergvall reveals the processes of literary and masculine individuation to be rooted in literary tradition (Goldstein 2009). Reading Bergvall via Erin Moure prompts me to reconsider 'Via' as an intranslation in its own right: understood by Moure as a process rather than a finished product, intranslation highlights the social dimension of translation by performing its own provisionality. What Moure calls and performs as 'intranslation' can thus be interpreted, via Bergvall's 'Via', as an invitation to creatively and critically engage with translation as a stage in which processes of subjectivity can be repeated while being side-stepped, translated without being reproduced.

3. **Performative translation is theory in practice:** As Moure argues, the relationship between perception and interpretation is not consecutive, nor is it clear-cut: 'we don't perceive, then interpret. Interpretation is an instantaneous shutter. The world is simultaneously perceived and framed. Seeing and hearing are never pure, never objective' (Moure 2009: 49). Equally, performative translation is an interpretive and investigative performance not only of a text but of translational conventions. It has the power to create, summon and/or breach referentiality at any moment, walking and subverting the line between reproduction and mimesis, translation and fiction. Performativity in translation does not simply invoke new forms of writing, but new critical ontologies which confound creativity and criticism. In that sense, performative translation is a future-oriented practice which summons new communities in invoking, fabricating or displacing their differences. It is in this sense that I propose to read Olympe de Gouges' rewriting of *La Déclaration des Droits de l'Homme et du Citoyen/The Declaration of the Rights of Man and Citizen* (1789) into *La Déclaration des Droits de la Femme et de la Citoyenne/The Declaration of the Rights of Woman and Citizen* (1791). When giving this text to read to students

on a first-year module on the French Revolution module I teach, they are often surprised, and sometimes alarmed, by her irruption in the space of another text: why did Olympe de Gouges choose to copy the text and add to it, instead of writing her own separate critique of it? De Gouges' intralingual translation of *The Declaration of the Right of Man and Citizen* was, of course, a way for De Gouges to symbolically intervene in the public sphere from which she is excluded. But as well as being an attempt to translate herself and other women into the sphere of universal political action which the *Declaration* delimits, her text is also an attempt to interpellate a new community of readers through the process of translation. For if translation is the act of translating a text from one linguistic community into another, Olympe de Gouges' *The Declaration of the Rights of Woman and Citizen* is a translation by dint of its effort to re-imagine the political community it addresses through the medium of translation. De Gouges' translation is therefore performative in the sense that *The Declaration of the Rights of Woman and the Female Citizen* inaugurates and acts out a community-to-come through the performance of translation.

Performative translations, as briefly explored in the examples above and as will be shown in more detail through the following exploration of Carson's translations of Sappho's fragments, can reveal the 'deep cultural performances' reproduced in translation as a form of citationality (Diamond 1996: 7). They are, as such, performances which raise to our consciousness the historical provisionality of translational forms and norms, making us aware, through their defamiliarising presence, of the structures which maintain unequal representations of language, cultures, genders and sexuality in the process of translational repetition.

Out-Translating Sappho

I now turn to Sappho to explore the extent to which Carson's translations of her works can be read as a creative-critical engagement with Sappho's reception. My aim here is not to provide an exhaustive account of Sappho's translation and mythologisation but to study some examples of Sappho being 'out-translated', or outperformed in translation. Sappho's translation, I will first argue in this sub-section, has often displaced Sappho from her own works, relocating the narrative of female desire in her texts within the masculine. Writers such as Catullus and philosophers such as Plato, as we shall see, have not hesitated to translate the 'I' of feminine desire in the texts into a masculine form.

Of course, like other ancient texts, what remains of Sappho's works exists in fragments and, to the extent that Sappho, as a performer, almost certainly did not write down her poetry herself, what remains of Sappho's text is also certainly second-handed to us. To read Sappho's fragments, even in the archives, is, inescapably, to read her entangled with her reception, to explore her works through this continuously absent presence. Beyond her translation and textual reception, moral anxiety regarding Sappho's sexual orientation and her life as a woman-poet have been the main point of focus of her reception: translations of Sappho's fragments, as well as her pictorial representations, have transformed Sappho into a muse and a warning for women-poets. Here, I want to open my analysis by presenting two contrasting visual representations of Sappho, before moving on to explore translations which have out-translated in her works. Both depictions of Sappho's art can be read as attempts to translate and mythologise her archival 'loss' in different ways. Both are also commentaries on Sappho's literary and cultural representations as a muse, rather than on what remains of Sappho's poetry.

The first is a portrayal of Sappho dating back to 1893 by Gustave Moreau (Figure 4). The painting depicts the legend of Sappho hurling herself off a cliff after her lover, Phaon, has departed.

Figure 4 Gustave Moreau, *Sappho*, 1893, oil on canvas, 85 × 67 cm

Moreau's representation of Sappho, whom he painted repeatedly between 1870 and 1893, depicts the story about the fatal leap of Sappho into the sea at the headland of Leukas as depicted in Ovid's elegiac poems *The Heroides*. In Ovid's tale, Sappho the author is turned into a mythological character alongside Medea, Ariadne and Dido. She is the antithesis of the more stoic and faithful Helen and served as a warning to many would-be female artists across the ages. For Moreau, her lyrical perdition is also her sexual perdition: she is a broken woman in both the physical and moral sense of the word. Here, a mythical Sappho is seen jumping off a cliff after her lover's departure. Her representation in his paintings is one of many efforts by visual artists to turn Sappho into a muse or goddess character, and therefore of absorbing her, an author and artist in her own right, into the fabric of his narrative of femininity.

The other is the Sappho entry which can be found in Monique Wittig and Sande Zeig's *Lesbian Peoples: Materials for a Dictionary* (1979) (Figure 5).

The entry on Sappho in Wittig and Zeig's *Lesbian Peoples* seems to acknowledge the absence of Sappho at the heart of her mythologisation (Wittig and Zeig 1979: 136). Of course, the blank space hints at the fact that all the material remnants of Sappho we have, whether in papyri or in reproduced lyrics used by grammarians across the ages, have been second-handed to us. Even when more

Figure 5 Photo of the Sappho entry, p.156 (left page), in Monique Wittig's and Sande Zeig's *Lesbian Peoples: Materials for a Dictionary* (1979)

papyri were discovered in Oxyrhynchus, Egypt at the end of the nineteenth century, critics continued to spend more time trying to locate her sexually than to study her poetry. For many nineteenth- and twentieth-century writers and scholars, it is Sappho's loss itself, her fragmentation, which fascinates. As noted by Margaret Reynolds: 'Like the battered torso of the Venus de Milo, her injuries repel, and yet the idealised perfection of the imagined whole inspires a nostalgia and a longing that are greater than those directed towards any other object of desire that is present, intact and accessible' (Reynolds 2010: 6). And indeed, the myth of Sappho's broken body and text has probably surpassed the literary attention that is paid to her fragmented works. The blank space thus reveals an ungraspable surface, a space without depth and is a mourning of the loss of Sappho on-her-own terms. But it can also be received as a critique of the eternal feminine with which Sappho has been associated. As revealed in Moreau's representation of Sappho's moral and physical 'fall', 'fictions of Sappho' (DeJean 1987) are also fictions of the feminine, stories of archetypal femininity from which both Sappho the poet and women in general, Wittig and Zeig seem to suggest, are absent.

Wittig and Zeig's resistance to fill the gap of Sappho's absence with myth is a powerful sign of the forms of lyrical dislocation with which Sappho's works themselves threaten patriarchal political discourses. Sappho's haunting of male-dominated practices and genres, as is explored in Adrian Kelly's study of Sappho's reappropriation of traditional Homeric epic genre for her purpose, has been seen as early as Plato and Catullus in Ancient Greece and Rome as a potential threat to the political order of the city (Kelly 2021). Their translations relocate Sappho outside of the city's walls but also outside of her own text: Sappho's authorship, in these examples, is challenged by the dominance of Plato and Catullus' voices which ventriloquise her poems.

The first example takes place in Plato's *Phaedrus*. When Socrates, in *Phaedrus*, discusses the importance of eros, the philosopher decides that this discussion must take place outside of the polis, during which Socrates, in a trance, translates parts of Sappho's 'Fragment 31' into prose in his own voice:

> Whenever he sees a godlike face which is a good imitation of beauty, or some bodily form, first he shivers and then something of that fear comes over him, and then, as he gazes on, he reveres him like a god . . . And as he looks at him, a change comes over him from the shivering, and sweat and unfamiliar heat grips him. For as he receives the emanation of beauty through his eyes, he heats up . . . (Plato 251ab, translated by Lyndsay Coo 2021: 268)

As noted by Lyndsay Coo, 'parallels have long been noted between this passage and Sappho's famous depiction of eros' in Fragment 31 (Coo 2021: 268).

Socrates does not directly acknowledge the provenance of this passage in *Pheadrus* but announces Sappho's influence on his thinking earlier in the text:

> Right now I am unable to say, but it is evident that I have heard something, either from the beautiful Sappho or the wise Anacreon or from one of the prose-writers. ... I know perfectly well that I have come up with none of these things myself, but there remains the possibility, I think, that I have been filled up through my ears by the flowing streams of another, like a pitcher; but again, owing to my stupidity, I have forgotten how and from whom I heard it. (Plato 235 cd, translated by Lyndsay Coo 2021: 266–7)

Let us reflect on what I would call Socrates' rhetorical forgetfulness here. How does it frame how we read Sappho's poetry? To what extent does the fragmentation of Sappho's voice by Socrates' descriptive translation act as a strategy of containment and interruption of her poetry's performative potential? As a result of only being able to access Sappho through the gates of Socrates' rhetorical forgetfulness, both poetry and Sappho are exiled from philosophy in two significant ways. First, Sappho's translation and critical conceptualisation of eros is metaphorically translated out beyond the city's walls. Second, the poetic dimension of her works, in other words, the potential impact of her words on readers, is contained by their re-narration into philosophical prose throughout the book. For Sappho's poetics of self and desire have influenced Plato, as vaguely acknowledged in Socrates' admission of forgetfulness, beyond this retranslated passage of her works. However, rather than allowing Sappho to speak in her name, her words are filtered by Socrates' memory and voice. In out-translating Sappho from her texts, Socrates' character is able to re-embody her narration of desire from a masculine perspective.

Socrates is not the only one to have outshone Sappho in their translation of her texts. The interception of Sappho's authorship in Plato's translation of Sappho is also adopted in Catullus' own translation and rewriting of 'Fragment 31' in 'An Imitation of Sappho: to Lesbia', here translated by A. S. Kline (Catullus 2001: 74). In this instance, Sappho's voice is interrupted by Catullus in the middle of the poem:

> He seems equal to the gods, to me, that man,
> if it's possible more than just divine,
> who sitting over against you, endlessly
> sees you and hears you
> laughing so sweetly, that with fierce pain I'm robbed
> of all of my senses: because that moment
> I see you, Lesbia, nothing's left of me .....
> but my tongue is numbed, and through my poor limbs
> fires are raging, the echo of your voice

rings in both ears, my eyes are covered
with the dark of night.
'Your idleness is loathsome Catullus:
you delight in idleness, and too much posturing:
idleness ruined the kings and the cities
of former times.'

(Sappho translated by Catullus and back-translated
into English by Kline 2001: 74)

Catullus translates and inserts himself in the very structure of the poem, interrupting Sappho's voice and intercepting the poem's disorienting impact on him as he does so. As noted by Ellen Greene, in Catullus' version, 'the figure of "that man" (ille) dominates the first stanza of the poem, whereas in Sappho's original, the man serves primarily to point up the contrast between the impassivity he exhibits and the speaker's highly charged emotional responses to the woman' (Greene 1999: 4). In thus translating 'Fragment 31', Catullus displaces the reader's attention from the speaker's self-perception of desire to her rival. In so doing, Catullus translates himself out of Sappho's lyrical influence, forestalling, as it were, the power of Sappho's poetry over the reader in the process. But in so doing Catullus also acknowledges the power of Sappho's poetry to threaten the political order of the city, an order which he tried to rescue by disciplining Sappho with his voice in the last stanza.

More than any other translator of Sappho, Catullus makes plain that her translation out of the archives is also a rescuing of normative order. A reordering of the 'arkheion': 'a domicile, an address, the residence of the superior magistrate, the *archons*, those who command' (Derrida 1995/1996: 2). The translator becomes the rescuer not of Sappho's own will to lose herself in the trance of desiring but also to loosen herself from the grips of a patriarchal order in which she does not want to be located. Both Plato's and Catullus' translations of Sappho's fragment 31 also become ways of legislating her works, displacing Sappho to the periphery of philosophical discourse by exiling her from political influence. Anne Carson's translations of Sappho, as we shall see, reframe the haunting of Sappho as a form of postmodern ghosting instead.

Anne Carson's Translation

Carson's translations of Sappho's works explore fragmentation as both the object of Sappho's poetic project and as a material practice of engagement with the text by making moments of silence between languages and within Sappho's fragments visible. In other words, her performative translation is also, in the 'performative' sense employed by Karen Barad, an 'inquiry on the practices or performances of representing' in translation itself (Barad 2007: 49).

Rather than filling the gaps or guessing at a poetic totality behind the fragmented archival materials, Carson performs instead the translator's desire for the source text through the framing and foregrounding of gaps, silences and absences in the target texts. Although the desire to make Sappho fully present in the text is acknowledged, it never realises completion: the translation, instead, is traversed and diffracted by the many silences present in the archives of her texts. She explains her aesthetic process as follows:

> When translating texts read from papyri, I have used a single square bracket to give an impression of missing matter, so that] or [indicates destroyed papyrus of the presence of letters not quite legible somewhere in the line. It is not the case that every gap or illegibility is specifically indicated: this would render the page a blizzard of marks and inhibit reading. Brackets are an aesthetic gesture toward the papyrological event rather than an accurate record of it. (Carson 2002: xi)

The empty brackets, rather than faithfully reproducing missing parts in the original, are crafted into the poem selectively and consciously, undergoing a translational and editorial attention in their own right. In so doing, Carson signs the archival temporality of the source text by writing what she calls the 'papyrological event' of the poems' disappearance into the very structure of her translations, allowing the reader to translate the silences and gaps along-side her. She explains: 'Brackets are exciting. There is no reason you should miss the drama of trying to read papyrus torn in half or riddled with holes or smaller than a postage stamp – brackets imply a free space of imaginal adventure' (Carson 2002: xi). Carson's citation frames translation as a 'process' rather than as a product. Her aim is not only to translate Sappho but to translate translating Sappho. It also reframes translation as a collective endeavour and 'drama': hers is a translation which invites other translations. It is, in the words of Moure, an invitation to intranslate: to explore the impossibility of 'not' translating Sappho, whose works, by dint of their fragmentation, can only ever be performed rather than known or 'captured' by poetry translation.

As a result of the aesthetic prominence given to the incompleteness of the source text, Carson's translations seem to be haunted by the lost figure of the original the translation is meant to anticipate and recreate, as if Sappho's fragments were commenting on their own archival disappearance. The theme of desire seems to perform the impossibility of translating the source text, or of even reaching the source. Desire, and thus the translator's subjectivity, is thus 'languaged' into the translational process as an active part in the reconstruction of the source text. In 'Fragment 31', for example, the shifting positionality of the pronouns typical of Sappho's works (duBois 1995: 137) is signified by the translator's hesitation:

> He seems to me equal to the gods that man
>
> whoever he is who opposite you
> sits and listens close
>   to your sweet speaking
> and lovely laughing – oh it
> puts the heart in my chest on wings
> for when I look at you, a moment, then no speaking
>   is left in me
> no: tongue breaks and thin
> fire is racing under skin
> and in eyes no sight and drumming
>   fills ears
> and cold sweat holds me and shaking
> grips me all, greener than grass
> I am and dead – or almost
>   I seem to me.
>
> But all is to be dared, because even a person of poverty
>   *(Sappho translated by Carson 2002: 63)*

In this translation, the framing of Sappho's fragmentation as something from which Sappho needs to be rescued in translation is complicated by the fact that this loss is something which is also willed by Sappho and etched within the structure of her own poetic testament. The 'I' of the poem wants to lose herself in the other woman she admires. The tension linking and fracturing 'me' and 'no', 'I am' and 'dead' at once is one way in which Carson performs the inherent contradiction between Sappho's performance of desire and the act of translating her: how to translate Sappho without betraying her desire to disappear in ecstasy?

Sappho's 'Fragment 31' is the object of much critical attention in Carson's writing. The poem represents a triangulation of desire between the speaker, a man and another woman. A man makes a woman laugh. Is she in love with him? While the man remains impervious to his effect on the woman sitting opposite him, the speaker watches the woman desiring the man and in turn desires the woman. At first glance, a love triangle seems to emerge from the scene. But in Carson's translation, the characters are not so much differentiated as they are diffracted into each other's presence. Carson's translation of the poem and her essays on 'Fragment 31' emphasise, above all, the role of geometry and perception, in other words, of optics, in the poem's representation of desire. This, Carson writes, is not a poem about jealousy, or even 'a poem about the three of them as individuals' (Carson 1986: 13). 'Fragment 31', she argues in *Eros the Bittersweet*, is 'about the geometrical figure formed by their perception of one another, and the gaps in that perception' (Carson 1986: 13). In *Decreation*, she goes further, explaining: Sappho's text is 'not just a moment of revealed existence: it is a spiritual event. Sappho enters into ecstasy' (Carson 2005: 161). *Ekstasis* in Ancient Greek, Carson explains, is the condition of 'standing outside oneself, a condition regarded by the Greeks as typical of mad persons, geniuses, and lovers, and ascribed to poets by Aristotle' (Carson 2005: 161). In the poem, Sappho disappears to simultaneously reappear into the diffracted motion of desire's mutlipositionality. As a movement of self-translation, 'ecstasy changes Sappho and changes her poem' (Carson 2005: 161). In that sense, to recover Sappho, to rescue her, in the way a translation would normally 'restore' an original to itself, would be to betray her.

Carson's version of the poem differs from other translations of this poem in its doubling up of the word and phenomenon of 'seeming'. While the first half of the poem is mostly dedicated to describing the object of desire central to its narrative scene, the second half seems to repeat it from the perspective of the speaker in the poem. This repetition is emphasised in Carson's version by the echo of 'I seem' in 'he seems' at the end of the poem, a form of visual semantic echoing which, although thematically present, does not exist as strikingly in the following translation by Mary Barnard:

> He is a god in my eyes –
> the man who is allowed
> to sit beside you – he
>
> who listens intimately
> to the sweet murmur of
> your voice, the enticing
>
> laughter that makes my own
> heart beat fast. If I meet
> you suddenly, I can't
>
> speak – my tongue is broken;
> a thin flame runs under
> my skin; seeing nothing,
>
> hearing only my own ears
> drumming, I drip with sweat;
> trembling shakes my body
>
> and I turn paler than
> dry grass. At such times
> death isn't far from me.
>
> *(Sappho translated by*
> *Barnard 1958/2019: 39)*

While syntactically defamiliarising in English, 'I seem to me' placed at the end of the poem in Carson's version closely resembles the repetitive structure of the poem in Ancient Greek. In her essay 'Just for the Thrill: Sycophantizing Aristotle's Poetics', Carson offers a critical reading of 'the problem of seeming' in the poem, which can inform our analysis of her translation:

> It is a strangely theatrical poem, as brightly lit as a stage set and much concerned with the problem of seeming. It begins and ends with a form of the verb phainesthai, 'to appear': phainetai (v. 1) 'he seems,' phainomai (v. 16) 'I seem'. Seeming is an activity that ordinarily posits a cast of two. The person who seems and the person to whom she seems. But on Sappho's stage the action is triangular, at least to begin with, for the opening stanza features three actors, 'that man' and 'you' and 'me'. And although Sappho immediately sets about reducing the cast to 'you' and 'me' in the second stanza and then 'me' alone in the remaining verses, phenomena double and triple themselves insistently throughout the poem. (Carson 1990: 149)

In what Carson describes as the brightly lit stage set of the poem, the activity of seeming seems to diffract the 'I' and translate the subject of perception. The boundaries between the internal and external world of the speaker collapse as the senses normally seaming and holding the body together come undone in the lyrical performance of unseeing. In the grips of desire, the body relearns itself through its differential becoming. The acting power of Eros is only heightened, as noted by Emily Wilson, by 'the lack of possessive pronouns or definite articles that are not in the Greek' (Wilson 2004) in Carson's translation, in which 'speaking', 'tongue', 'skin', 'eyes' and 'ears', in other words, the speaker's five senses, seem to attain a form of agency as actors in the scene. This individuation of the senses as the self's agents of chaos is, for example, not present in the more linear trajectory of Barnard's translation. In this version of the poem, desire is a linear unfolding which the self can articulate and order through the use of possessive pronouns. Carson's translation of Fragment 31, however, is an exploration of seaming and seeming, of the mutual implication of knowing and being through the figure of Eros where to see or to perceive become performatively unmeshed in the stage of one's own disappearance.

Like Simone Weil, Carson argues in her essay 'Decreation: How Women like Sappho, Marguerite Porete and Simone Weil Tell God', Sappho 'had a program for getting the self out of the way which she called Decreation'. By comparing Sappho's poetic project to Weil's theological program, Carson reinvents Sappho as the agent of her own disappearance. She writes: 'We see her senses empty themselves, we see her Being thrown outside its own center where it stands observing her as if she were grass or dead' (Carson 2005: 176). Perhaps, Carson posits, Sappho's poem poses a 'spiritual question': 'What is it that love dares the self to do? Daring enters the poem in the seventeenth verse when Sappho uses the word "tolmaton": "is to be dared"' (Carson 2005: 177). This last line, although incomplete, is omitted in most translations of Fragment 31. Mary Barnard's translation, for example, ends with:

> and I turn paler than
> dry grass. At such times
> death isn't far from me.
> *(Sappho translated by Barnard 1958/2019: 39)*

In 'Decreation', Carson seems to theorise her own translation project from the viewpoint of this very last line. To paraphrase Carson when she speaks about Sappho, what is it that the translator, as a lover of Sappho's texts, dares herself to stay true to; Sappho's ecstatic practice? The translation, it seems, dares, 'to enter into poverty' (Carson 2005: 162). Carson, in other words, dares to perform the absence of Sappho in translation, and to reinvent what translating is. Rather than intimating a form of completion or original behind the texts, and therefore 'redeeming' Sappho, Carson re-invents translation to translate Sappho's performance of *being* as being *with*, as a sympoetic gesture.

In Carson's translation, Sappho is not so much haunting her fragments as 'ghosting' her readers. Sappho's haunting is not only the result of archival fragmentation but the product of Sappho's own decreation in the text. Carson is thus not translating an original in fragments: but the very lack of an original, fixed 'I' at the source of Sappho's texts. Take, for example, this translation of Sappho's 'Fragment 55' by Chris Childers:

> You'll lie low when you're dead, and be forgotten by posterity.
> No one will think of you with love, who never plucked the roses of
> Pieria; in Hades' hall, you'll be, as here, invisible,
> and flit about, where none can mark, among the corpses in the dark.
> *(Sappho translated by Childers 2019)*

In Childers' translation, the narrator of the poem is addressing another woman, threatening her with posthumous anonymity. In Carson's version of Sappho 55, however, the narrator of the poem seems to be addressing herself in a quasi-autotheoretical gesture:

> Dead you will lie and never memory of you
> will there be nor desire into the aftertime – for you do not
> share in the roses
> of Pieria, but invisible too in Hades' house
> you will go your way among dim shapes. Having been breathed out.
> *(Sappho translated by Carson 2002: 115)*

In Carson's version, Sappho's invisibility to Hades is empowering: allowing her to be '[going her] way' having been 'breathed out', liberated rather than captured by Carson's performative translation of her fragments. Performing Sappho *in* translation, Carson rewrites Sappho's epitaph as the agent of her own 'ghosting' from the archives. In so doing, she symbolically writes Sappho out of the influence of the 'Archōn' of masculine authority.

Conclusion

Performative translations invite us to pay as much attention to what is translated as to how it is translated, and the ways in which the how, that is, the practice of translation itself, can be mobilised in the performance of interpretation and theorisation. They function as a mode of experimental criticism which can rewrite seemingly unmediated forms and question the hidden desires within our translational intentions. Rather than a simple process of demystification on the fictions of translation, they encourage us to engage with translation practice and criticism by performing their own translational method. More than a process between two pre-existing material points, it seems, performative translations interpret source and target cultures as unstable, changeable places which translation can transform. Translation, in this performative context, is explored as a continuous zone of creative-critical performance, of communal 'deformation' and reformation of accepted norms of linguistic and cultural differences (McSweeney and Göransson 2012).

Carson's translations of Sappho are a case in point of what I have tentatively defined as performative translation. Her translations of Sappho explore the presence-absence of the source text in translation, performing the veiling and unveiling of the text and its transformation by signing gaps and silences of the archive in the text. In so doing, her translations open a breach within the text's illusion of presence to allow the text to address the present through a different historical and cultural lens. Playing on the 'when' and 'where' of her translated text, her translations invite a wider critical and ethical reading of textual manipulation in translational rewriting and demonstrate the possibility of performing the theme of desire omnipresent in the source text through the poetics of translation failure. To perform the epistemological limits of her translation and her desire as a translator is thus a way for Carson to question the historical and ideological density of translation as a fiction of restitution and retrieval of the original.

3 Transtopias

I often open my module 'Translation as Creative Critical Practice' by showing students short clips from *Des Voix dans le Chœur'*, Henri Colomer's beautiful documentary of translators at work (Colomer 2017). I ask them this simple question: what do translators do? In the documentary, we see translators often poised between two texts, one the translation, the other the target text. We see translators reading texts out loud in one language, then another language. We see them speaking to themselves in different languages – muttering, stuttering and finally moulding new works out of this intense process of reading and writing in translation. Indeed, translators are often portrayed as intercultural experts, as go-betweens and diplomats busy with the complex task of suturing the gaps of comprehension between cultures. In this vision of translators as 'bridges' and 'negotiators', translators are seen as more or less passive transmitter of messages whose roles are active only in so far as they may use their skills to best render meaning between two fully fledged, official expressions of these cultures. In this context, as Venuti's works in particular have well documented, the labour of translators is often occulted, made invisible (Venuti 2019). But what possible geographies and non-exclusive forms of belonging are banished by exiling translators and translations from the cognitive map of literary production?

As we know, both translation and fiction are the purveyors of particular geographical imaginations. Benedict Anderson shows, for example, that 'novels create a form of spatial temporality in which the very idea of a united nation and a people is possible' (Anderson 1983). Translation scholars have also demonstrated that translation is an important conceptual tool in structuring literary and geographical imaginaries in ways which settle national communities or strengthen racial or cultural prejudice (Sakai 2009, 2017; Samoyault 2020). Naoki Sakai, for example, convincingly argues that more than a 'bridge' between fully fledged nations and borders:

> translation can inscribe, erase, and distort borders; it may well give rise to a border where none was before; it may well multiply a border into many registers; it may erase some borders and institute new ones. Similar to the manoeuvre of occupation in war, translation deterritorializes languages and probable sites of discommunication. It shows most persuasively the unstable, transformative, and political nature of border, of the differentiation of the inside from the outside, and of the multiplicity of belonging and non-belonging. (Sakai 2017: 106)

And indeed, historically, the work of creating new borders has also been accompanied by performative acts of translation meant to reinforce or introduce new differences between new nation states, often adding layers of linguistic and cultural complexity to the national spaces they have tried to separate. Recently, Sherry Simon's *Translating Sites: A Field Guide*, a work which seeks to 'identify and describe sites of translation', where 'languages compose ever-changing palimpsests and where spaces are charged with the tension between here and elsewhere', has also opened new avenues for thinking spatial relations in translation (Simon 2019: 2). Hers and Sakai's works stand out in demonstrating the conceptual limitations of thinking that translation is an act performed between distinct cultures and monolingual nations. I want to argue here, by leaning on these works and Lisa Samuels' text 'The Right to be Transplace', that what is banished in invisibilising translators is a particular 'transtopian' point of view and perception which can be made visible by translation practices. Explaining the term 'transplace' as a deconstruction of the ideology of 'Fromness' and the 'dominant narrative of single-place origin' (Samuels and VanHove 2020: i2), Samuels locates her 'Fromness' and that of other transplace people within movement itself. She writes:

> Setting to one side for now the important topics gestured to by the term transnational, transplace as movement states that when movement happens between one body/place and another, the movement itself is a real condition of being. Transnational assumes identifiers based on nations, thus it conditions, albeit in interesting political ways, what transplace might mean. Here transplace means to resist and side-step, to exceed and differentiate from nation-state identification. . . . Movement is a real substance; its in-between of bodies in places is another instance of thinking the heft and breath of the in-between. To be transplace is to be as from, to be shaped in the absence of unique place-origin and in the presence of multiple movement-origin, many kinds of fromness. (Samuels 2018: 245–6)

Samuels' articulation of transplacement involves the act of disorienting nationalist frameworks and maps of literary production. To be transplace, then, is to be not at home spatially and ontologically in the framework of identification provided by the nation. Transplace in the sense that Samuels uses it means to be actively engaged in mattering/muttering different geographies of being.

In this Section, I will build on these works to explore what I will call 'transtopias': translation art and literary translations which use experimental forms of translations to challenge normative representations of place and identity funnelled by the nation. Transtopias, I will argue, create and perform theoretical positions from which to explore the critical and creative potential of translation to build and imagine alternative geographies of being and belonging. Although the term echoes the term 'utopia', transtopias as I understand them are not an invitation to override existing conflictual geographies of power or to uncritically conceive of translation in utopian terms. As creative-critical endeavours, they are provisional fictional places of contestation and critique where new forms of being-in-the-world may be intimated. Performing artistically what may be called intentional 'contact zones' where, as Pratt put it, 'cultures, meet, clash and grapple with each other, often in contexts of highly asymmetrical relations of power' (Pratt 1991: 34), transtopias put to work the polysemic and dialogic spaces which translation often produces to create a counter-poetic space to cultural hegemonies. In this sense, transtopias are creative-critical explorations of what Homi Bhabha (1994/2012) identified as the translational process located in the 'third space' of culture. For Bhabha, 'the process of translation is the opening up of another contentious political and cultural site at the heart of colonial representation' (Bhabha 1994/2012: 49) – a site of hybridity which, far from being a space of linguistic play beyond material concerns, functions as a radical questioning of the 'utopianism of a mythic memory of a unique collective identitiy' (Bhabha 1994/2012: 50).

While traditional translation norms tend to reify the immanence of the source text and culture, transtopias visibilise translation and the translator to matter, weave and perform into poetic existence the space between national cultures. In so doing, they show that what exists between nations and cultures is not a 'spacey emptiness' (Spivak 1993: 180) between two destinations, but a place full of matters and that matters, a somewhere already filled with things, people and objects. To show this, I will reconsider translation not as primarily an act of transmission between pre-existing cultures, but as an act of spatial expansion and imagination, a 'worlding' capable of summoning into existence forms of lives which have been traditionally erased, negated or alienated from the canonical archives of national literary cultures. Examining examples of creative-critical use of translation in film, visual art and literature, I will ask: what happens when we turn to translation practice as a place of 'translocation' and geographical subversion?

We Are We by Noémi Lefebvre, Laurent Grappe and Sophie Lewis

During an event I organised for Lancaster Litfest (UK) entitled 'Found in Translation: Literary Dispatches from the Peripheries of Europe' (2019), I invited several writers and translators from different European locations to work together on the theme of the 'periphery'. Each wrote a text on this theme, bearing in mind recent populist framings of 'peripheries' through which Brexit was presented as a counter-hegemonic discourse (Salter 2018). After each had produced a text, they translated each other's works from languages they did not necessarily know. Emma MacGordon, for example, translated a poem by Grigory Semenchuk (Ukraine) using sound translation and the only word (in fact a car brand) she understood from Semenchuk and Sandig's recorded performance of 'Lexus'.[4] The result was an exchange, in the form of translation, on the kinds of places and locations which translation could materialise. But it

---

[4] https://landschaft.bandcamp.com/track/lexus.

Figure 6 Extract from Ines Labarta's *On Peripheries* (2019)[5]

was also a performative homage to the forms of accidental meanings produced by dint of performing one's work in a multilingual space. This curational intention was narrated by Ines Labarta (2019) in a comic strip (Figure 6).

[5] www.meits.org/blog/post/translation-as-performance-in-found-in-translation-literary-dis patches-from-the-peripheries-of-europe.

My request to all performers that they translate each other's works meant that everyone was actively included in the building of a temporary performative space at the interstices between languages and cultures. Beyond each individual work, this participative curatorial space became a work in its own right – a cartography, in translation, which existed beyond each individual production, as mapped above by Ines Labarta's drawing. The multi-layered process of translation therefore self-reflexively explored curation as a translational action in its own right. A 'work of relation' ('mise en relation'), in other words, producing its own 'cognitive cartography' ('cartographies cognitives') (Imhoff and Quirós 2015: 2).

As well as a translation, film, music and writing performance, then, 'Found in Translation: Literary Dispatches from the Peripheries of Europe' became a translational performance in its own right: a space where each practitioner was able, through the use of translation, to imagine a new spatial and linguistic relation to one another's work. As curatorial practice, 'Found in Translation', then, could be described as an effort to map alternative ontographies (Latour 2012) through the subversive use of translation.

One of the pieces produced for the event was a French text and film by Noémi Lefebvre and Laurent Grappe which was given the English title *We are We* (Lefebvre and Grappe 2019).[6] The dialogue is made, partly, of translated extracts from a British newspaper into French on the subject of Brexit. While the dialogue between the characters, played by Lefebvre and Grappe, is replete with topographical descriptions and semantic localisation, the text itself makes no reference to specific countries. Instead, the characters attempt to locate their cultural identity through tautological description. Here is an extract of the text in French, followed by the translation by Sophie Lewis, a literary translator of Noémi Lefebvre's novels into French:

—Nous en faisons partie
—Absolument
—C'est la réalité
—Ça a toujours été
—Mais nous ne sommes pas dedans
—Absolument pas
—Nous n'avons jamais été vraiment dedans même quand nous y étions
—Nous y étions mais sans en être
—Nous y étions mais en partie seulement.
—Parfois les gens nous demandent « mais comment ça se fait que vous ne voulez pas en faire partie alors que vous dites que vous en faites partie ? »

---

[6] https://wordswithoutborders.org/read/article/2019-04/we-are-wereflecting-on-nationalist-discourse-through-film-noemi-lefebvre/.

—Ils se demandent comment c'est possible alors ils nous demandent
—Nous leur disons que nous en faisons partie, en effet, mais que nous ne voulons
    pas être dedans puisque nous n'y sommes pas.
—C'est pourtant clair.
—Nous ne sommes pas en dehors
—Tout en étant pas dedans
—Cette façon d'être, en y étant tout en n'en étant pas, c'est tout nous.
—C'est tout nous, d'être nous.
—C'est comme ça
—Ça a toujours été
—We are part of it
—Absolutely
—That's the way it is
—It always has been
—But we are not within it
—Absolutely not
—We have never been truly within it even when we were
—We were in but without being of it
—We were in but only in part
—Sometimes people ask us 'But how is it you don't want to be part of it when you
    say that you are part of it?'
—They wonder how that's possible so they ask us
—We tell them that we are indeed part of it, but that we don't want to be within it
    since we aren't
—Actually it's quite clear
—We are not on the outside
—Even while not being within it
—This way of being, being of it even while not being of it, that's so us.
—It's so us to be us
—That's how it is
—It always has been
    (Lefebvre and Grappe, translated by Sophie Lewis, 2019)

A frequent feature of political discourse supporting the 'leave vote' such as 'Brexit means Brexit' or 'Leave means Leave', 'tautology is typically used in linguistics to refer to a statement that is true concerning every possible situation. This is achieved through the repetition of the same lexical or propositional content (e.g. boys will be boys, a deal is a deal)' (Mompean and Valenzuela Manzanares 2019). In the context of *We are We*, tautology is used as a form of ontological assertion from which is derived an entire logic of communication and perception. Tautology, in this sense, almost seems to function ideologically by thwarting the possibility of dialogue through its performative epistemic enclosure. *We are We*, in this sense, vocalises the unchangeable and therefore inscrutable nature of British identity. Paradoxically and inevitably, however, in attempting to apply tautological discourse to explain their position on Brexit to others beyond the 'we', the characters break several cooperative principles of communication. According to Grice:

> Our talk exchanges do not normally consist of a succession of disconnected remarks, and *would not be rational if they did*. They are characteristically, *to some degree at least, cooperative efforts*; and each participant recognizes in them, to some extent, a common purpose or set of purposes, or at least a mutually accepted direction. (Grice 1975: 45, italics in the original)

Contrary to this principle, the solipsism of 'we are we' is deployed in the dialogue between the two characters to justify seemingly contradictory claims: the fact of being within Europe and outside of it, 'a part of it'/ but 'not within it', 'in'/ but 'not of it', 'in'/ but only 'in part'. Inaccessible to others beyond the 'we' which claims to be only graspable to the speaker, the meaning and referentiality of 'we' is revealed to be nonetheless quite slippery. The more the characters attempt to pinpoint this 'we', however, the more the characters' logic of self-localisation undermines and undercuts itself. *We are We*, for one, is grammatically stilted in English: a language which prevents this kind of personal pronominal tautology. To achieve this form of self-tautology *We are We* has to have recourse to a grammatical 'calque', or translation procedure, based on the grammatical structure of the French 'nous sommes nous', therefore applying a foreignisation procedure to realise itself.

The adaptation of the text into a film spoken in French by two protagonists further highlights the impossibility of nationalist discourses to narrate their identity without translating and traducing itself by its own standards. To a French ear and pronounced with a French accent, the 'we' pronounced 'oui' (French for 'yes'), further destabilises the narrative of national exception which the characters of the short film engage with (Figure 7). Beyond the impossibility to contain language and meaning within one national language, this highlights the necessity to step outside of oneself to begin to understand oneself.[7]

As a creative performance, this multi-layered translation, first from English into French, and then from French into English, provides the viewer with a provisional space for thinking the colonial and ethno-nationalist undertones of discourses surrounding Brexit at the time. It is transtopian in the sense that it matters, through the critical and deconstructive lens of translation, a provisional space of parodic performance between the two languages and cultures, thereby exposing the discursive solipsism of ethno-nationalist discourse as impossible to maintain within the cooperative parameters of communication. In this

---

[7] A still from *We are We* https://wordswithoutborders.org/read/article/2019-04/we-are-wereflecting-on-nationalist-discourse-through-film-noemi-lefebvre/.

Figure 7 Noémi Lefebvre and Laurent Grappe in a still from *We are We* (2019)

context, translation's theoretical gaze deconstructs, in practice, the linguistic self-enclosures of national and cultural distinction, alerting us to the degree of self-translation already inherently present in such tautological discourses. For is not the 'we', in 'we are we', already a form of intralingual translation? To say 'Brexit means Brexit' is always to translate 'Brexit' into something else that can never be exactly repeated a second time. *We are We* thus opens ethno-nationalist discourse to a model of translation as practice-based research, one capable of debunking the pseudo-realism of ethnocentric language.

Slavs and Tatars

The vast and multifaceted engagement of artist collective Slavs and Tatars with cultural and linguistic translation offers a historically aware reflection of translation's role in maintaining the appearance of natural communities. Founded in 2006, Slavs and Tatars self-describe as 'a faction of polemics and intimacies devoted to an area east of the former Berlin Wall and west of the Great Wall of China known as Eurasia'.[8] Mixing different media as well as cultures, 'the collective's practice is based on three activities: exhibitions, books and lecture-performances' which cross the boundaries between creative and art criticism. As a counter-spatial movement which seeks to transcend binary spatial constructions between East and West, Slavs and Tatars' spatial translations involve not only transcending symbolic identity structures but epistemological norms through cultural and linguistic translation. Their lecture performances, art

---

[8] https://slavsandtatars.com/about.

installations and (re)writings explore forms of knowing and spatial constructions which decentre Western forms of localisation and theorisation.

As part of their work cycle entitled 'Région d'être' ('Regions of being', but also a play on the French 'raison d'être', or 'existential purpose'), for example, Slavs and Tatars explored cultural practices of reading across Iran and Central Asia. This particular work cycle, they explain,

> spans the unwieldy geographical remit of Slavs and Tatars – between the former Berlin Wall and the Great Wall of China – while also serving as a prequel to the collective's practice. Régions d'être is the collective's term for an area that falls between the cracks of history and general knowledge: largely Muslim but not the Middle East, largely Russian speaking but not Russia, and having a complex relationship with the nation. Yet rather than representing a specific value, history or culture, this 'region of being' is as much an imagined, poetic geography as it is a real, political and historical geopolitics.[9]

As a transtopian project both in its use of language(s) and approach to geographical space, *Region d'être* adopts a provisional and situated approach to knowledge, translating, creatively and critically across media and cultures, the architectures of practice underpinning cultural knowledge productions. Their works model a translational approach to reading where reading is never done in cultural isolation, but always in the presence of others. Echoing Edouard Glissant's multilingual philosophy of relation, this non-isolationist practice of reading and understanding culture and languages in the presence of others reframes difference as a methodology of knowledge in such a way that translation itself becomes a research methodology. For example, their work *RiverBed* (2017), inspired by the Iranian 'takht' (sofa or long bench), a piece of furniture on which to read or take a break together, revisits the solitary experience of reading in the West from a Central Asian perspective.[10] As an intervention into how we collectively think and practice reading in Western Europe, *RiverBed* opens the practice of reading to transtopian geographies where, in the words of Bakhtin, 'truth is not born nor is it to be found inside the head of an individual person, it is born between people collectively searching for truth, in the process of their dialogic interaction' (Bakhtin 1984: 110). Encouraging us to think of reading as a social and dialogic space, *RiverBed* symbolically projects reading into the generative and experimental space of translation.

Part of the same work cycle which exposes some of the theoretical articulation of their collective artistic practice, their work series *Kitab Kebab*, is another

---

[9] https://slavsandtatars.com/cycles/regions-d-etre.
[10] https://slavsandtatars.com/cycles/regions-d-etre/riverbed.

material investigation into the embodied practices of reading in translation (Figure 8). In this installation,

> a traditional kebab skewer pierces through a selection of Slavs and Tatars' books, suggesting not only an analytical but also an affective and digestive relationship to text. The mashed-up reading list proposes a lateral or transversal approach to knowledge, an attempt to combine the depth of the more traditionally-inclined vertical forms of knowledge with the range of the horizontal.[11]

As a metaphor for textual interaction, *Kitab Kebab* (which translates from Arabic as a 'book kebab') eschews transcendental approaches to knowledge to perform a 'horizontal', permeable practice of reading and writing, proposing, instead, a transversal reading practice (from the Latin 'trans': across or beyond). *Kitab Ketab*, then, signifies the Slavs and Tatars' practice of reading one book in the presence of other books, one culture in the presence of other cultures, as *En Islam Iranien* suggests. The books in the various reproductions of this series,

Figure 8 *Kitab Kebab* (*En Islam Iranien*), 2013, books, metal kebab skewer, 50 × 60 × 40 cm

---

[11] https://slavsandtatars.com/cycles/regions-d-etre/kitab-kebab.

many of which are translations, combine and explore writings on or about Middle Eastern and European modernity. Their exploration of cultural hybridity exposes rather than hides the performative role of translation in the construction of difference, creating multilingual objects and spaces which can be read multi-directionally as well as multiculturally. The simultaneous gaze hinted at in the name of Slavs and Tatars is one which always aims to translate and ethnogra-phise in both directions, thereby creating transtopian spaces where no one is the other's other.

As well as cultural transtopias, Slavs and Tatars use linguistic and script conversion to investigate the multicultural and linguistic archives of Eurasian nations. Their artistic project series and lecture performance 'Transliterative Tease', for example, explore the transliteration of alphabets of 'Turkic lan-guages of the former Soviet Union, as well as the eastern and western frontiers of the Turkic sphere, namely Anatolia and Xinjiang/Uighuristan'.[12] Using 'the lens of phonetic, semantic, and theological slippage', this work series examines 'the potential for transliteration – the conversion of scripts – as a strategy equally of resistance and research into notions such as identity politics, coloni-alism, and faith'.[13] Inviting us to reflect on the translational archives of these national languages, Transliterative Tease hybridises the historical and cultural boundaries of nations by highlighting their translated beginnings.

Dig the Booty, for example, 'features a transliteration of an aphorism across the Latin, Cyrillic and and Perso-Arabic scripts in homage to the vicissitudes of the Azeri alphabet which changed 3 times over the past century: from Arabic to Latin in 1929, from Latin to Cyrillic in 1939, only to go back to Latin in 1991'[14] (Figure 9).

In their lecture 'Satire and the Muslim World: Molla Nasreddin' (Slavs and Tatars 2015), Slavs and Tatars define transliteration as: 'language in drag: it's essentially language, putting on the clothes of the other. If transla-tion is a form of linguistic hospitality, to take Paul Ricoeur's word, translit-eration is a form of language in drag; it's wearing the outfit of the other'(2015). In *Dig the Booty*, their transliteration of the sentence defies the more traditionally ethnographising gaze of translation by putting the cultures of three scripts in historical and cultural relation. Moreover, the sexual allusion in the text denaturalises the stable couple monolinguism/ nation by displaying the theatrical props of national sovereignty through its layers of (re)iteration across time and space.

---

[12] https://slavsandtatars.com/lectures/the-tranny-tease.
[13] https://slavsandtatars.com/lectures/the-tranny-tease.
[14] https://slavsandtatars.com/cycles/kidnapping-mountains/dig-the-booty.

Figure 9 *Dig the Booty*, 2009, vacuum-formed plastic, acrylic paint, 64 × 91 cm

As artistic research into forms of embodiments in nationalisation processes, this work is a transtopian tribute to the fact that, while Azeri have had to ideologically conform and pledge exclusivity to one empire or culture at a time, their country was multilingual and multiscriptural in practice. In other words, national conquests and politics of assimilation cannot avoid the following paradox: the more a country is assimilated and nationalised, the more multilingual it, at least historically, becomes. Paying attention to how practice can shift traditional narratives of self-knowledge, unsettles them, teases them even, *Dig the Booty* is a perfect case in point of how a practice-based approach to translation can denaturalise the concept of nation and create alternative frameworks of being and belonging. Revealing the processes of nationalisation to be full of 'mimicry' and 'slippage', this work highlights the paradoxes of monolingualism as a constructed and often oppressive form of self-introspective and orientation (Bhabha 1994/2012).

We are We and Slavs and Tatar's queering of the location of culture through the parodic use of translation and transliteration echo, in more than one way, Homi Bhabha's articulation of the third space as a way of rewriting oppressive identity discourses from the margins of established national identities. Writing from a post-colonial perspective, Bhabha argues that translational slippages allow for dissenting and minority voices to claim a degree of agency within colonial structures of identity production. For Bhabha:

> we should remember that it is the 'inter' – the cutting edge of translation and negotiation, the inbetween space – that carries the burden of the meaning of culture. It makes it possible to begin envisaging national, anti-nationalist histories of the 'people'. And by exploring this Third Space, we may elude the politics of polarity and emerge as the others of our selves. (Bhabha 1994/2012: 56)

This happens, in colonised nations, when colonised subjects' imitation of colonising cultures expose their internal contradictions. This third space, Bhabha argues optimistically, opens up a space for new communal imaginary. Transtopian creative-critical translation practices apply such practices knowingly and performatively. Like Bhabha's post-colonial third space but in a context where the British imperialistic gaze is applied to Europe, *We are We* rearticulates difference from within their parody of self-translation, while Slavs and Tatars, on the contrary, explore self-exile and transliterative 'drag' to analyse and critique the homogenising performativity of national cultures. In different ways, their technique relies on applying translation untraditionally and subversively. Their work is translational in the curatorial sense of the term described by Aliocha Imhoff and Kantuta Quirós as a 'pratique de l'interstice' ('intersticial practice'). Their translational task is also their curatorial task: to open up new spaces of translation beyond pre-established differences, to thicken holes and inconsistencies in self-solipsistic discourses and to (hopefully) recover political agency beyond the entrenched connection between the self and the same.

Paratextual Transtopias: Chantal Wright's Translation of Yoko Tawada's *Portrait of a Tongue*

I now turn to forms of translated fictions which have played with paratextual tropes of translation practice as a way of thickening not the source text's language but the translation process itself. In so doing, I want to argue, translators become the fictional writers of new psycho-spatial geographies. Rather than applying ready-made spatial concepts to read and understand translation, they encourage us to stay with the trouble of translating, to unearth and research the in-between spaces traditionally unmapped by pre-established literary canons and geographical grand-narratives. In this context, as we shall see, paratextual transtopias are a symbolic intervention, through the visual spatialisation of the source text on the page, on the national and cultural geographies reproduced in the abstract myth of authorial agency.

An important way of mediating how translations are read and received, Gérard Genette, describes the paratext as

> what enables a text to become a book and to be offered as such to its readers and, more generally, to the public. More than a boundary or a sealed border, the paratext is, rather, a threshold, or – a word Borges used apropos of a preface – a "vestibule" that offers the world at large the possibility of either stepping inside or turning back. It is an "undefined zone" between the inside and the outside, a zone without any hard and fast boundary on either the inward side (turned toward the text) or the outward side (turned toward the

world's discourse about the text), an edge, or, as Philippe Lejeune put it, "a fringe of the printed text which in reality controls one's whole reading of the text." (Genette 1997: 1–2)

As a space of mediation between fiction and the world, the paratexts, then, mediate and delimit the relationship between reading and writing, writing and translating. The paratext, in other words, is also what constitutes what is inside and 'off-text', or outside of the domain of literary writing 'proper'. As both Katheryn Batchelor and Şehnaz Tahir Gürçağlar have astutely shown, however, Genette's definition of the paratext as subordinate to the text has implications for how we value translation in literature (Tahir Gürçağlar 2002: 46; Batchelor 2018: 28). For Tahir Gürçağlar, 'the implications of this statement for translation research are clear. They mean that translation, when regarded as paratext, will serve only its original and nothing else' (Gürçağlar 2002: 46). In the context of translation, then, paratexts are traditionally enlisted to reinforce the division between the translator's voice and the author's, but also between source culture and target culture. What queer literary geographies of belonging and literary production are occulted in the process? While Venuti has already highlighted 'the ethnocentric violence' committed 'by domesticating translations', what I want to attend to is the erasure of translation as a location of culture which the canonical fiction of national literary fields reinforces by performing the interiority and exteriority of languages and cultures (Venuti 2019, 39). In this subsection, which explores recent paratextual experiments in creative-critical translation practice, my aim will be not so much to enlist the visibility of the translator in order to restore the authenticity of the source culture and nation, but to explore the paratext as a transtopian literary space capable of queering geographies of belonging. I will do so by comparing the ideological posture of Vladimir Nabokov's annotated translation of *Eugene Onegin* with Chantal Wright's paratextual translatopia in her translation from German into English of Yoko Tawada's novella *Portrait of a Tongue*.

Described by Kwame Anthony Apiah as a 'translation that seeks, with its annotations and its accompanying glosses, to locate the text in a rich cultural and linguistic context', thick translations can better our understanding of the source culture from which source texts emerge (Apiah 1993: 817). Translation notes, in this context, offer a pedagogical tool in raising the cultural awareness of readers to different literary, cultural and historical tradition by bringing speakers of dominant languages closer to the source language and culture. Nabokov's approach to translating *Eugene Onegin* combines the use of 'translation notes like skyscrapers' to an aspiringly literal translation of the source text (Nabokov 1955/2021: 155). His use of notes is a well-researched example of a paratextual practice used to 'thicken' translation in order to make visible the source text and culture.

Used to capture and restore the source text in the target language, his translational process entailed closely translating the source text from Russian into English and accompanying his translation with as many notes as necessary in order to bridge the missing, or untranslatable aesthetic dimension of the source text. He explains:

> I want translations with copious footnotes reaching up like skyscrapers to the top of this or that page so as to leave only the gleam of one textual line between commentary and eternity. I want such footnotes and the absolutely literal sense, with no emasculation and no padding – I want such sense and such notes for all the poety in other tongues that still languishes in "poetical" versions, begrimed and beslimed by rhyme. And when my Onegin is ready, I will either conform exactly to my vision or not appear at all. (Nabokov 1955/ 2021: 155)

Using unmistakably phallocentric language and imagery, Nabokov portrays alternative forms of rhymed translation as a violation not only on the original sense of text but on the sovereignty of the author. Consequently, Nabokov's individual notes endeavour to delimit the critical and authorial inviolability of Pushkin's writing, performing what he sees as what ought to be the boundaries of translation's reproductive imagination. His understanding of translation produces the fantasy of translation as a purely 'utilitarian prose' (Nabokov 1957/1989: 201), and through it, the fantasy of Pushkin's 'universal and divine' canonicity (Nabokov 1955/2021: 117).

Nabokov limits translation to what he considers to be the borders of the literary text and, moreover, the borders of the Russian language. His version of literalness is an idealised version of a scientific approach to translation, as indicated in this translation allegory in 'Problems of Translation: Onegin in English': 'Short of its primary verbal existence, the original text will not be able to soar and sing; but it can be very nicely dissected and mounted, and scientific- ally studied in all its organic details' (Nabokov 1955/2021: 119). In this nod to his past as a lepidopteral specialist, Nabokov likens his translation approach to that of studying a fixed specimen: the process of translation becomes that of fixing the original in the source culture. In a stark variation of what Benjamin thought of as the afterlife of the original, the source text becomes ossified by the translation process and thereby, of ossifying the source culture (Benjamin 1923/ 2021). The use of translation, in this context, is used not only to broaden and educate anglophone readers into other cultures but to perform and reinforce the immanence of individual works and languages along nationalist and patriarchal notions of authorship and reproduction. In so doing, Nabokov professes to resist what he puts strikingly as 'the queer world of verbal transmigration' (Nabokov 1941/1981: 315).

Eschewing such Modernist concerns and nostalgia for authorial transcendence, contemporary creative-critical translations invite a more playful, postmodern relation with paratexts in general. Anne Carson's poetic use of paratext in *Nox* (2009), Christina MacSweeney's translation of Valeria Luiselli's *The Story of My Teeth* (2015) and Chantal Wright's translation of Yoko Tawada's *Portrait of a Tongue* (2013) to name a few examples, reorient the paratext as a space of readerly and translational participation. Rather than dismissing the transmigratory as anti-intellectual in Nabokov's fashion, they explore the spaces and geographical orientations materialised and yet often unexplored in translation practice. They turn the space between cultures into a place of dwelling and thinking, opening our mental maps to historical and political counter-geographies of existing linguistic and cultural status quos. What could be qualified as a form of paratextual 'transmesis', which Beebee coined to 'refer to literary authors' use of fiction to depict acts of translation', is self-reflexively adopted by translators rather than authors to question the boundary between writing and translating (Beebee 2012: 3). As we shall see, both Wright and MacSweeney's respective collaborations with Tawada and Luiselli harness the creativity of fiction to perform the material presence of the presence of the translator as a co-creator of the text. As such, such works unsettle the impermeability of national literature to translation, and reveal the process of circulating literature to be dialogically and narratively complex.

My first example on the road to paratextual analysis is MacSweeney's translation of Luiselli's *La historia de mis dientes* (2015) into *The Story of My Teeth* (2015), a novel which tells the story of Gustavo Sánchez Sánchez, a Mexican auctioneer nicknamed 'Highway' who auctions off historical figures' teeth such as Plato, Virginia Woolf and Petrarch. Commissioned for Galería Jumex in Ecatepec, Luiselli wrote the novel by submitting chapters for 'lectores' to read to Jumex factory workers. The author then wrote her following chapters by taking the factory workers' recorded discussions into account. The catalogue, which describes the artistic project and exhibition Luiselli's novel was a part of, explains:

> With an eye toward reconsidering the role of the curator as translator or mediator, we decided first to create a report of the facts as they occurred within the context of the factory and the exhibition space. We asked Ignacio Perales, vocalist of Los Pellejos and a professional claims adjuster, to prepare a brief, objective report of the exhibition as it appeared before the viewer's eyes. We then invited Valeria Luiselli to imagine a story that could narrate

how the artworks that comprise this exhibition communicate between themselves and with the environment that surrounds them.[15]

Mirroring this brief and wider collaborative artistic project it stemmed from, Luiselli's English translator MacSweeney proceeds to take on the role of curator of the novel. As well as translating the novel into English, MacSweeney expanded Luiselli's work in a curatorial fashion by adding a chapter consisting of a timeline at the end of her novel, listing dates of events in Mexican and world politics, art and literature. This translational gesture can be read as a nod to the novel's collaborative beginnings: the novel's structure, in this sense, mirrors the cooperative working structure of the factory it originated from. Moreover, I am also tempted to read MacSweeney's pseudo-academic fact-checking exercise as a pun on the English translation of the Spanish 'fabrica' (factory). Extending the curatorial comment above, what we are given to read in the additional chapter is a 'fact-story', a story made up of pseudo-facts and exercises which writes the paratext, a space normally dedicated to academic fact-checking, into the domain of fiction. In fictionalising the paratext in this pseudo-historical comparative exercise, MacSweeney's fact-story reminds us that history, too, can be a space of invention and fictionalisation. The presence of the translator in the text therefore materialises translation as a space of rewriting and therefore retelling of histories as well as stories. They remind us that reading translations of 'foreign' texts risks flipping our mental maps and histories of the world on their head, but also of (mis)appropriating others in the process.

Wright's translation of Tawada's *Portrait of a Tongue* is also case in point of such experimental paratextual practice. Her translation is divided into two parts: the translation of *Portrait of a Tongue* into English on the left, and Wright's running commentary of both source text and translation on the right. Wright's experimental approach to translation is explained as follows on the back cover of the translated novel:

> Since the text invites the reader to interact with it – to go to the dictionary, for example, or to think about why a particular linguistic phenomenon appears odd to the narrator – and since the text often does not complete its own thoughts, a translation that acknowledges and embodies this interaction between the text and the reader-translator, as well as acknowledging and embodying the text's new geographic and linguistic environment, seems both an appropriate and a creative approach. (2013: book jacket)

The interactive dimension of Wright's translation is authorised, according to Wright, by the translatedness of the original as well as the creative geographies it embodies. A bilingual writer in German and Japanese whose playful writings

---

[15] www.fundacionjumex.org/en/explora/publicaciones/8-el-cazador-y-la-fabrica.

reflect on the formal structures of language(s), Tawada is known for challenging the stability of monolingual frameworks of meaning production. In her study of Tawada's bilingual writing, Yasemin Yildiz explains that Tawada's turn to language is 'a response to the problematic inclusion into the monolingual paradigm'. Yildiz traces what she designates as the monolingual paradigm back to the eighteenth century, and specifically in the German Romantic period, to the works of Friedrich Schleiermacher's essay 'On the Different Methods of Translating'. She writes:

> The monolingual paradigm arising in the eighteenth century gradually, but radically, changed this framework and put the – assumedly singular – native language and ethno-national identity of the writer into the forefront, until it became unimaginable for many to write in anything but their 'mother tongue'. To return to a key phrase, Friedrich Schleiermacher asserted in 1813 that "every writer can produce original work only in his mother tongue, and therefore the question cannot even be raised how he would have written his works in another language" ("On the Different Methods" 50). As Schleiermacher's emphasis on "original work" indicates, this attitude derives from a particular conception of originality and creativity rooted in authenticity, with authenticity in turn deemed possible only in a singular native language. (Yildiz 2013: 112)

Yildiz rightly roots the construction of the mother tongue paradigm in the particular family romance of the nation, which used the terms mother-tongues and fatherlands to naturalise monolingualism to the point of seeing as alien other forms of language constructions. In her works, Tawada engages with language and writing not only from the perspective of multilingualism but from the perspective of translation as the origin of all speech and communication.

As already explored in many scholarly articles dedicated to Tawada's works, far from an afterthought, translation is already implicated at the very 'translational poetics' of her writing and preoccupation with language (Brandt 2014: 181). Throughout her works, and through a form of writing which is defamiliarising to native German readers, her fictions are fictions of and about language which continually deconstruct structures of looking and thinking within language through the process of literary and cultural translation. In her study of surface translation in Tawada's works, Susan Anderson argues for example that 'Translation for Tawada shows that language is not a tool for transmitting meaning, but it is an integral part of meaning production' (Anderson 2010: 53). For Tawada indeed, translation is not only the source but the language of creativity and critical thinking. Her fictions interpellate modes of being which lie outside of the pre-supposed 'natural communities' of national languages.

The first-person narrator in *Portrait of a Tongue*, whom readers may suppose is a fictional version of Tawada as a writer, follows the trajectory of P., a woman whose language, after living in the United States for many years, has become inflected by English. It is a portrait of a woman and of a language in translation, and through the proliferation and disseminating power of her linguistic mistakes, of the disorienting impact of this translation on the narrator, who starts to see and measure her mother-tongue language through the mechanical tropes and turns of thoughts encoded in its translated, Americanised version. Throughout the novella, the narrator relates the woman's mistakes and reflects on them in a way that makes her question her own mechanical thought processes in German, reorienting her and the narrative continuously through the inadvertent literary translations of P's German from English:

> It was the day of my event at the Goethe-Institut in Boston. P phoned and asked, *"Wollen wir die Fahrt miteinander teilen?"* At first I didn't understand what she was trying to say. The word teilen made me think of the cost of the journey and confused me. In the course of our conversation it turned out that P wanted me to go with her in her car. Other people would have said: *"Soll ich dich im Auto mitnehmen?"* or *"Soll ich dich dahin fahren?"* How awkward the usual formulations sound compared with her offer! The expression that P had used was influenced by American English. But that didn't change the fact that we really did share this journey with one another. The fact that I reached my destination more quickly and more comfortably was of no importance. P gave me the feeling that we were sharing a piece of time with one another. (Tawada translated by Wright 2013: 57–8. Italics in the original.)

Both in her critical introduction to her method and in practice, Wright similarly places her translation within a cognitive stylistics framework where, quoting Jean Boase-Beier in her introduction, 'it is the nature of the literary text to invite creative engagement' (Wright in Tawada 2013: 29; Boase-Beier 2006: 55). She explains: 'My prose translation seeks out that space – which has always been open to translators of poetry – located between enslavement to the original and the creation of a text that is so loosely inspired by the source text that it is no longer, strictly speaking, translation' (Chantal Wright, in Tawada 2013: 29). Her definition of 'translation-with-commentary' highlights the commentary as 'an integral part of the translation' (Chantal Wright, in Tawada 2013: 30). Wright's creative-critical engagement with the translation commentary creates a territory for the thinking and creative process of translation. Unlike Holmes' translation studies map, this creative-critical territory is one where thinking and practicing translation are deeply entangled.

Wright's translation can be described as performative insofar as her translation imitates what Tawada's text does with language as well as what it says.

Beyond the element of performance inherent to her staging her translation via the medium of her reflexive commentary, her paratextual experiment is a playful manner to process the thinking of her doing and the doing of her thinking. An acknowledgement of the disorienting power of Tawada's literary text onto monolingual literary paradigms, Wright's translation continues the work of disrupting the national geographies of literary production by allowing her translation to intervene at the moment in which a translation might risk transforming the source text into an original in the traditional sense of term. Indeed, Tawada's novel is 'born-translated' in the most obvious sense (Walkowitz 2015), since it reads as a translation commentary in its own right. In the novel, the first-person narrator, whose first language we do not know except that she speaks German, not only analyses the quirks of the English language but the quirks of the German language from the generative perspective of P's anglicised German. P's literal translations of English into German, in other words, have for effect to denaturalise the thinking structures of both languages at once. In this narrative context, Wright's translation of Tawada's text and her translation commentary does not so much seem to explain as to mirror its narrative content:

I looked up the word 'greyhound' in
my dictionary and found two transla-
tions of *Windhund*   [Literally, wind-dog; this is the German
                                           term for all dogs classified as sight-
                                           hounds; the greyhound breed which
                                           belongs to this group is usually referred
                                           to by the English word 'greyhound']

                                           . . .
                                           (Tawada/Wright 2013: 49–50. Italics
                                           in the text.)

Here, Wright's translation commentary on the right seems to continue Tawada's own language commentary on the left. The break normally existing between the narrator's voice and the translator's presence in translation notes is therefore not as clear-cut as normally appears. The linguistic reflections and anecdotes in the source text appear mirrored in Wright's translation commentary, foregrounding the fiction of translation as a transparent linguistic process. Wright's translation expands the creative gesture of the source into new territories and geographies of writing, highlighting in a manner similar to MacSweeney's additional chapter to Luiselli's novel, the fictional promise and possibilities opened up by translation practice.

   As well as mirroring Tawada's own linguistic commentary in the source text, rhizomatic autofictional narrative shoots seem to be activated by the act of translation, giving the impression of a continuous dialogue between the first-person fictional character and the translator's fictional voice:

P hakte sich bei mir ein, it was raining,
and we had only one umbrella. In
America one rarely touches the bodies
of people of the same sex. I missed the
touching, I missed Berlin.

[P put her arm around mine]
In North America people excuse
themselves in supermarkets if they get
too close to you as they walk down an
aisle. I realized after several months
that impatiently reaching past
somebody to get something off a shelf
could be construed as rude. My
mastery of the art of packing shopping
bags quickly and expertly – acquired
in Vienna and Berlin, where dallying
has consequences – was now
a redundant skill. Nobody is in a rush
and there is usually somebody around
to pack your bags for you.

(Tawada/Wright 2013: 104–5. Italics
in the text)

Here, Wright not only gives us an extension or thickening of the source text but provides a different point of view on the matter discussed in the source text. In this performative dialogue between the first-person narrator of *Portrait of a Tongue* and the autofictional voice of Wright as translator, I cannot help but return to the tautological 'we' imagined by Lefebvre in *We are We*. In rewriting their together-ness through each other, both narrator and translator perform another manner of being *with* each other that does not warrant either assimilation or exclusion. Both MacSweeney and Wright's paratextual experiments, instead, subvert the hierarch-ies implicit in ideologies of national belonging in a way which invites us to read *interstitially*. Wright's performative translation, in other words, is one which thickens the historical connection between the subject and the object of translation, acknowledging that 'there can be no simplistic, essentialist opposition' between original and translation, the self-same and the other (Bhabha 1994/2012: 38). In so doing, they also geographically disorient, in the manner of the meandering gaze provoked by Wright's commentary (from left to right and right to left), our geographical orientation towards the nation, mattering and muttering a mental and creative territory beyond our imagined national existences. In this sense, all transtopias explored in this chapter encourage us to a form of 'travel reading': they push us to experiment with new territories of existence and belonging and to imagine new geopolitical contexts. In so doing, creative-critical translations also act as a creative-critical geography.

Conclusion

Like literary monuments, works commonly understood as 'literary originals' embody an idealised whole in the context of the modern nation and act as a powerful site of imagined collective immanence binding individuals to communities and communities to individuals. We project onto them the responsibility of binding disparate communities, cultures and languages: they are, in short, how writing is translated into the symbolic order of (national) identities. Transtopian works such as I have explored excavate these temporal geographies in such a way as to make visible the paradoxes inherent to translation conceived as the management of stable, pre-existing differences. They show instead that translation can be critically harnessed to introduce 'différance', negotiation and critical thinking on site of their repro-ductions (Derrida 1972/1982). These thoughts lead me to one last artwork I have recently come across, and which seems to me to both offer a striking image of such contestations and dispel any notion of such transtopian spaces as uncritical utopias. I am referring to *Palianytsia*, a stone culture by Ukrainian artist Zhanna Kadyrova (Figure 10).

A 'palianystia / паляниця' is a Ukrainian type of bread difficult to pro-nounce by Russian speakers. It has been used by Ukrainians as a shibboleth to

Figure 10 Zhanna Kadyrova. *Palianytsia*. 2022. Fundraising project for Emergency in Ukraine. Castello 2145, Riva San Biasio, 30122 Venice. Photo: Natalka Diachenko

identify Russian soldiers who invaded Ukraine during the invasion of their country. In this sculpture, Palianytsia is turned into an intersemiotic translation of its newly acquired meaning during the war: that of an unwelcomed, imperialist invasion of one country by another. As an anti-imperialist gesture, the stone material used to create this work materially signifies the undigestible nature of the invaded country. Subverting translation's reputation for hospitability, this translation creates a semiotic border between the two cultures by materially performing its resistance to translation as a weapon of colonial subjugation. That this space of contestation and critical reappraisal of translation happens *in* practice is crucial to the forms of theorising of identity production which this kind of works intimates. As a creative-critical approach to geographies of belonging, transtopias remind us that, far from simply being the act of bridging existing differences, translations can also inaugurate, contest and rewrite pre-existing differences. They infuse translation with the responsibility of mattering and re-conceptualising identity and difference beyond the discursive enclosure of 'fromness' (Samuels 2018) by keeping the practice of translation open for ethical renegotiation.

Conclusion

If, as Sakai argues, translation makes and sustains differences and hierarchies between languages, nations and cultures, translators can, by resisting simplistic frameworks of differences, decreate, multiply and desystematise the classifications of difference imposed on their practice. Far from an anti-intellectual gesture, then, deconstructing the relationship between translation practice and translation theory in translation studies is thus a call to open translation to more, not less, critical thinking. By calling into question not only the epistemological norms which govern translation but the field of translation studies as a discipline, my aim is to inspire renewed activity in translation as a field of political and theoretical engagement through practice. I have tried to show that 'weakening' the relationship between creative writing and theory, creative practice and critique in translation allows the translation memoir as autotheory to inaugurate new subject positions from which translators can speak as practice-led researchers and theoreticians of their works. In the second Section, I have explored how performative translations question the limits of theory by performing their own translatedness, arguing that translating within a pre-existing theoretical framework, performative translations performatively test the validity of these frameworks in the process of translating. Finally, I have explored the concept of transtopia in contemporary translation practices. I have shown how, by thickening the very process of translation rather than the source culture, transtopian works can critique and re-imagine ontologies of belonging within contexts of national and imperialist domination. Overall, I have tried to show that reframing translation practice as not only a norm-governed but as a world-making and geographically imaginative activity allows us to theorise translation failure as a site of cultural production and resistance. It is to open translation to wider epistemological conceptualisation and theoretical applications beyond its communicative model in international contexts.

While this Element's methodology has been to analyse various forms of creative-critical engagements with translation, much of my thinking has been inspired by explorations of translation as creative-critical practice in the classroom and as a translation dissertation supervisor. What might be the advantages of teaching translation as creative-critical practice? How can we change our pedagogical approach to translation in such a way as to embrace a practice-led approach to translation criticism? I will use one example to show how our pedagogical approaches might be reconsidered to accommodate a more dynamic relation between applied translation and translation theory through creative-critical practice.

Final-year translation dissertations are a staple of many undergraduate language courses in the UK. Instead of researching a literary, historical or political topic pertaining to their language study, students translate a text, which they usually accompany by translation notes and a translation commentary. In the commentary, students are encouraged to explore translation theories which have inspired their translation choices, allowing them to position their translation choices in a wider cultural and theoretical context. A potential problem with this translation dissertation model is that students often reproduce a top-down approach between theory and practice in their methodology section. In other words, the structure of the dissertation and the typical separation between translation practice and theory in the teaching of translation can mislead students into thinking that theory is something which can simply be 'applied' to translation practice as a way of injecting a form of higher thinking into their practice. The possibility of adopting a creative-critical approach to the translation dissertation might allow them to consider how experimenting with translation practice may test certain theoretical a-priori notions about translation. Self-reflective pedagogical approaches by scholars such as Paulina Pietrzak have already heralded the need to develop 'metacognitive skills' in translation training practices (Pietrzak 2019). I believe creative-critical approaches to translation might contribute to this pedagogical shift even further. As an example of what a creative-critical dissertation may look like, here is an abstract from one of my final-year translation-dissertation students, Martha Harwood:

Inspired by the translational practices that Clive Scott and Cecilia Rossi advocate, I propose a relatively creative and subjective translation based around a personal interaction with my selected text, Antoine de Saint-Exupéry's *Courrier Sud*. This involves using the Think-Aloud Protocol (TAP) to record the translation thought process and incorporate an individual response to the text into my final translation. The stream of consciousness style that is encouraged by the TAP was also partly inspired by my reading of Kate Briggs' *This Little Art*, which documents the personal psychological response triggered by the source texts of her translations. In order to combine these elements of translation I decided on using my own 'skopos'. This skopos framework sets out that my translation will use the TAP and creative reading and re-writing to produce a translation that is both a reflection of the source text, and a personal, phenomenological interpretation. I decided that this involves translating the source text's prose into poetry. I argue that it is possible to find a balance between an individual interpretation of a text, like those that Scott creates, and a text that is accessible to a new reader.

In her dissertation, we agreed that Harwood would research the possibility of translating *Courrier Sud* into verse, using a version of the TAP method in the process of doing so. In her translation commentary, she will be able to analyse the aesthetic and ethical consequences of doing so. Her approach will also allow her to explore the relationship between prose and poetry in the wider context of translation by potentially using reader-response theories as a method of analysis.

One may object that such an approach might encourage students to take too many liberties with the text and to lose sight of their responsibilities as translators altogether. But such an exercise must be understood as practice-based research into wider aesthetic and theoretical concerns in translation rather than as a form of linguistic test. Moreover, my experience of interaction with language and translation students undertaking such translation dissertations is that allowing them room for experimentation only heightens their sense of responsibility towards the texts they are translating and the theories they are exploring. Only when we realise the power of translation to redraw our a-priori understanding of difference, that is, when we have fully grasped the performative power of translation as a world-making exercise, will the urgency of such pedagogical changes be comprehended. By advocating for the pedagogical applications of translation as creative-critical practice in our current curriculum, my proposition is not to reverse current theoretical models of translation but to transform the one-way street of translation criticism into a multidirectional relationship between theory and practice.

References

Althusser, L. (1971/2008). *On Ideology*. Translated from the French by Ben Brewster. London: Verso.

Anderson, B. (1983). *Imagined Communities: Reflections on the Origin and Spread of Nationalism*. London: Verso.

Anderson, S. (2010). Surface Translations: Meaning and Difference in Yoko Tawada's German Prose. *Seminar: A Journal of Germanic Studies* 46(1), 50–70.

Anzaldúa, G. E. (1987). *Borderlands/La Frontera: The New Mestiza*. San Francisco: Aunt Lute Books.

Appiah, K. A. (1993). Thick Translation. *Callaloo* 16(4), 808–19.

Apter, E. (2006). *The Translation Zone: A New Comparative Literature*. Princeton, NJ: Princeton University Press.

Aru, E. (2010). When Translating Becomes a Ludic Activity. *Opticon1826*, 8, 1–7. https://student-journals.ucl.ac.uk/opticon/article/id/924/.

Aru, E. (2017). The Shadow's Skin. *Transartation!* www.youtube.com/watch?v=qo_IcDpvOTQ.

Austin, J. L. (1962). *How to Do Things with Words*. Cambridge, MA: Harvard University Press.

Bakhtin, M. M. (1984). *Problems of Dostoevsky's Poetics*. Translated and edited by Caryl Emerson. Minneapolis: University of Michigan Press.

Baltrusch, B. (2018). Sobre Tradutibilidade e Intradutibilidade em Walter Benjamin: On Translatability and Intranslatability in Walter Benjamin. *Florianópolis* 38(2), 32–60.

Barad, K. (2007). *Meeting the Universe Halfway: Quantum Physics and the Entanglement of Matter and Meaning*. Durham, NC: Duke University Press.

Barthes, R. (1975). *Roland Barthes par Roland Barthes*. Paris: Seuil.

Barthes, R. (1977a). *Fragment d'un discours amoureux*. Paris: Seuil.

Barthes, R. (1977b). *Journal de deuil*. Paris: Seuil.

Barthes, R. (1980). *La Chambre claire: Note sur la photographie*. Paris: Gallimard.

Barthes, R. (2002/2005). *The Neutral*. Translated by Krauss Rosalind E. and Hollier Denis New York, NY: Columbia University Press.

Barthes, R. (2002/2013). *How to Live Together*. Translated by Kate Briggs. New York, NY: Columbia University Press.

Barthes, R. (2003/2011). *The Preparation to the Novel*. Translated by Kate Briggs. New York, NY: Columbia University Press.

Barton, P. (2021). *Fifty Sounds*. London: Fitzcarraldo.

Bassnett, S. (2008). Writing and Translating. In S. Bassnett and P. Bush, eds., *The Translator as Writer*. London: Routledge, pp. 173–83.

Batchelor, K. (2018). *Translation and Paratexts*. London: Routledge.

Batchelor, K. (2022). Unsettling Translation: Paratext, Hypertext and Metatext. *Unsettling Translation*. London: Routledge, pp. 48–61.

Beebee, T. (2012). *Transmesis: Inside Translation's Black Box*. London: Palgrave Macmillan.

Benjamin, W. (1923–2021). The Translator's Task. Translated from German by Steven Rendall. In L. Venuti, ed., *The Translation Studies Reader*. London: Routledge, pp. 89–97.

Bennett, K. (ed.) (2020). *Intersemiotic Translation and Multimodality*. *Translation Matters* 1(20) https://ojs.letras.up.pt/index.php/tm/issue/view/475.

Benson, S. and Connors, C. (eds.) (2014). *Creative Criticism: An Anthology and Guide*. Edinburgh: Edinburgh University Press.

Bergvall, C. (2003). Via. In J. Osman and J. Spahr, eds., *Chain* 10, 55–9.

Berman, A. (1982/1992). *The Experience of the Foreign: Culture and Translation in Romantic Germany*. Translated by Stefan Heyvaert. Albany, NY: State University of New York Press.

Berman, A. (2000/2021). Translation and the Trials of the Foreign. Translated by Lawrence Venuti. In Lawrence Venuti, ed., *The Translation Studies Reader*.

Bermann, S. (2014). Performing Translation. In S. Bermann and C. Porter, eds., *A Companion to Translation Studies*. Chichester: John Wiley, pp. 285–96.

Bernstein, C. (2003). A Test of Poetry. Translated by Haroldo de Campos, Leevi Lehto, Ernesto Livon-Grosman and Traduction Collective à Royaumont. In J. Osman and J. Spahr, eds., *Chain* 10, 20–38.

Bernstein, C. (2015). 'Truth in the Body of Falsehood': Ian Probstein interviews Charles Bernstein on 9/11, translation, and amorality. *Jacket 2*. https://jacket2.org/commentary/probstein-bernstein-911.

Bhabha, H. (1994/2012). *The Location of Culture*. London: Routledge.

Boase-Beier, J. (2006). Loosening the Grip of the Text: Theory as an Aid to Creativity. In E. Loffredo and M. Perteghella, eds., *Translation and Creativity: Perspectives on Creative Writing and Translation Studies*. London: Bloomsbury, pp. 47–56.

Bourdieu, P. (1973). Cultural Reproduction and Social Reproduction. Translator unknown. In R. Brown, ed., *Knowledge, Education, and Cultural Change*. London: Tavistock, pp. 71–112.

Brandt, B. (2014). The Bones of Translation: Yoko Tawada's Translational Poetics. In L. Minnaard and T. Dembeck, eds., *Challenging the Myth of Monolingualism*. Amsterdam: Brill Rodopi, pp. 181–94.

Briggs, K. (2017). *This Little Art*. London: Fitzcarraldo.

Briggs, K. and LaRue, M. (2017). Waiting Translations: A Conversation with Kate Briggs. *Music & Literature*. www.musicandliterature.org/features/2017/11/20/a-conversation-with-kate-briggs.

Butler, J. (2012). *Parting Ways: Jewishness and the Critique of Zionism*. New York, NY: Columbia University Press.

Butler, J. (2019). Can't Stop Screaming. In S. Marcus and C. Zaloom, eds., *Think in Public: A Public Books Reader*. New York, NY: Columbia University Press, pp. 381–92.

Campbell, M. and Vidal, R. (2019). *Translating across Sensory and Linguistic Borders: Intersemiotic Journeys between Media*. London: Palgrave Macmillan.

Carson, A. (1986). *Eros the Bittersweet*. Princeton, NJ: Princeton University Press.

Carson, A. (1990). 'Just for the Thrill': Sycophantizing Aristotle's 'Poetics'. *Arion: A Journal of Humanities and the Classics* 1(1), 142–54.

Carson, A. (2002). *If Not, Winter: Fragments of Sappho*. London: Virago.

Carson, A. (2003). *If Not, Winter: Fragments from Sappho*. London: Virago.

Carson, A. (2005). *Decreation: Poetry Essay, Opera*. New York, NY: Random House.

Carson, A. (2009). *Nox*. New York, NY: New Directions.

Cassin, B. (2004). *Dictionnaire des intraduisibles*. Paris: Le Seuil.

Cassin, B. (2014). *Dictionary of the Untranslatable*. Translated by Michael Wood. Princeton: Princeton University Press.

Catullus, G. V. (2001). *Catullus: The Poems*. Translated by A. S. Kline. Web: Poetry in Translation. www.poetryintranslation.com/inc/unzip/unzip.php?filename=Catulluspdf.zip.

Chesterman, A. (2009). The Name and Nature of Translator Studies. *Hermes: Journal of Language and Communication Studies* 42, 13–22.

Chesterman, A. and Wagner, E. (2002). *Can Theory Help Translators?: A Dialogue between the Ivory Tower and the Wordface*. London: Routledge.

Colomer, H. (2017). *Des Voix dans le Chœur: Éloge des Traducteurs*. France: Saraband Films.

Coo, L. (2021). Sappho in Fifth- and Fourth-Century Greek Literature. In P. Finglass and A. Kelly, eds., *The Cambridge Companion to Sappho*. Cambridge: Cambridge University Press, pp. 263–76.

DeJean, J. (1987). Fictions of Sappho. *Critical Inquiry* 13(4), 787–805.

Derrida, J. (1972/1982). Différance. Translated by Alan Bass. *Margins of Philosophy.* Chicago, IL: University of Chicago Press, pp. 3–27.

Derrida, J. (1995/1996). *Archive Fever.* Translated by Eric Prenowitz. Chicago, IL: University of Chicago Press.

Diamond, E. (1996). *Performance and Cultural Politics.* London: Routledge.

duBois, P. (1995). *Sappho is Burning.* Chicago, IL: University of Chicago Press.

Felski, R. (2015). *The Limits of Critique.* Chicago, IL: University of Chicago Press.

Fournier, L. (2021). *Autotheory as Feminist Practice in Art, Writing and Criticism.* Cambridge, MA: MIT.

Genette, G. (1997). *Paratext: Thresholds of Interpretation.* Translated by Jane E. Lewin. Cambridge: Cambridge University Press.

Gepner, C. (2019). *Traduire ou perdre pied.* Paris: La Contre allée.

Glissant, E. (1990/1997). *Poetics of Relation.* Translated by Betsy Wing. Ann Arbor, MI: University of Michigan Press.

Godard, B. (1991). Performance/Transformance: Editorial. *Tessera* 11, 11–18.

Goldstein, L. (2009). Translation as Performance: Caroline Bergvall's 'Via'. *HOW2.* Arizona: State University Web. www.asu.edu/pipercwcenter/how2 journal/vol_3_no_3/bergvall/goldstein-translation-performance.html.

Gómez, I. (2018). Anti-Surrealism? Augusto de Campos Untranslates Spanish-American Poetry. *Mutatis Mutandis: Revista Latinoamericana de Traducción* 11(2), 376–99.

Greene, E. (1999). Re-Figuring the Feminine Voice: Catullus Translating Sappho. *Arethusa* 32(1), 1–18.

Grice, H. P. (1975). Logic and Conversation. In P. Cole and J. Morgan, eds., *Syntax and Semantics,* vol. 3. New York, NY: Academic Press, pp. 41–58.

Grunenwald, N. (2021). *Sur les bouts de la langue: Traduire en féministe/s.* Paris: La Contre allée.

Haraway, D. (2016). *Staying with the Trouble: Making Kin in the Chthulucene.* New York, NY: Duke University Press.

Hatim, B. and Munday, J. (2004). *Translation: An Advanced Resource Book.* London: Routledge.

Hermans, T. (1996). Norms and the Determination of Translation: A Theoretical Framework. In R. Álvarez and M. Carmen-África Vidal, eds., *Translation, Power, Subversion.* Clevedon: Multilingual Matters, pp. 25–51.

Hermans, T. (2007). *The Conference of Tongues.* London: Routledge.

Hilevaara, K. and Orley, E. (2018). *The Creative Critic: Writing as/about Practice.* London: Routledge.

Hjorth, B. (2014). We're Standing in/the Nick of Time. *Performance Research* 19(3), 135–9.

Holmes, J. S. (1972). The Name and Nature of Translation Studies. In J. Qvistgaard, ed., *Third International Congress of Applied Linguistics* (Copenhagen, 21–26 August 1972). Congress Abstracts, Copenhagen: Ehrverskøkonomisk Forlag. www.eric.ed.gov/PDFS/ED074796.pdf.

Imhoff, A. and Quirós, K. (2015). Curating Research: Pour une diplomatie entre les savoirs. *L'Art même* 58, 3–5.

Jackson, S. (2015). *Tactile Poetics: Touch and Contemporary Writing.* Edinburgh: Edinburgh University Press.

Johnston, D. (2013). Professing Translation: The Acts-in-Between. *Target: International Journal of Translation Studies* 25(3), 365–84.

Kadiu, S. (2019). *Reflexive Translation Studies: Translation as Critical Reflection.* London: UCL Press.

Karpinski, E. (2012). *Borrowed Tongues: Life Writing, Migration, and Translation.* Waterloo: Wilfried Laurier University Press.

Kelly, A. (2021). Sappho and Epic. In P. Finglass and A. Kelly, eds., *The Cambridge Companion to Sappho.* Cambridge: Cambridge University Press, pp. 53–64.

Kosofsky, E. S. (1997/2003). Paranoid Reading and Reparative Reading, or, You're So Paranoid, You Probably Think This Essay Is about You. In *Touching Feeling: Affect, Pedagogy, Performativity.* New York: Duke University Press, pp. 123–51.

Labarta, I. (2019). *On Peripheries.* www.meits.org/blog/post/translation-as-performance-in-found-in-translation-literary-dispatches-from-the-peripher ies-of-europe.

Latour, B. (2012). L'universel, il faut le faire: Entretien réalisé par Élie During et Laurent Jeanpierre. *Critique* 11(786), 949–63.

Lee, T. K. (2022). *Translation as Experimentalism: Exploring Play in Poetics.* Cambridge: Cambridge University Press.

Lefebvre, N. and Grappe, L. (2019). We Are We. Translated by Sophie Lewis. *Words without Borders*, 26 April 2019. https://wordswithoutborders.org/read/article/2019-04/we-are-wereflecting-on-nationalist-discourse-through-film-noemi-lefebvre/.

Loffredo and M. Perteghella, eds. (2006). *Translation and Creativity: Perspectives on Creative Writing and Translation Studies.* London: Bloomsbury.

Luiselli, V. (2015). *The Story of My Teeth.* Translated by Christina MacSweeney. Croydon: Granta.

Malmkjær, K. (2020). *Translation and Creativity.* London: Routledge.

McSweeney, J. and Göransson, J. (2012). *Deformation Zone: On Translation.* New York, NY: Ugly Duckling Presse.

Meur, D. (2019). *Entre les rives: Traduire, écrire dans le pluriel des langues.* Paris: La Contre allée.

Mompean, J. A. and Valenzuela Manzanares, J. (2019). Brexit Means Brexit: A Constructionist Analysis [Brexit means Brexit: un análisis construccionista]. *Complutense Journal of English Studies* 27, 1–37. https://doi.org/10.5209/cjes.64263.

Moure, E. (2009). *My Beloved Wager: Essays from a Writing* Practice. Alberta: NeWest Press.

Moure, E. (2021). *Elisa Sampedrín and the Paradox of Translation, or The Intranslatable.* Montréal: Zat-So Productions.

Moure, E. and Pato, C. (2014). *Secession/Insecession.* Translated by Erin Moure. Montréal: Book Thug.

Munday, J. (2016). *Introducing Translation Studies: Theories and Applications.* Fourth Edition. London: Routledge.

Mussgnug, F., Nabugodi, M. and Petrou, T. (eds.) (2021). *Thinking through Relation: Encounters in Creative Critical Writing.* Oxford: Peter Lang.

Nabokov, V. (1941/1981). The Art of Translation. In F. Bowers, ed., *Lectures on Russian Literature.* New York: Harcourt Brace Jovanovich, pp. 315–21.

Nabokov, V. (1955/2021). Problems of Translation: *Onegin* in English. In L. Venuti, eds., *The Translation Studies Reader.* London: Routledge, pp. 143–55.

Nabokov, V. (1957/1989). Vladimir Nabokov to Katharine A. White, 16 February 1957. In D. Nabokov and M. Bruccoli, eds., *Selected Letters 1940–1977.* New York, NY: Harcourt Brace Jovanovich and Bruccoli Clark Layman.

Nelson, M. (2009). *Bluets.* New York, NY: Wave Books.

Nelson, M. (2015). *The Argonauts.* Minneapolis, MN: Graywolf.

Nelson, M. and McCrary, M. (2015). Riding the Blinds. *LA Review of Books.* https://lareviewofbooks.org/article/riding-the-blinds/.

Nikolaou, P. (2006). Notes on Translating the Self. In E. Loffredo and M. Perteghella, eds., *Translation and Creativity: Perspectives on Creative Writing and Translation Studies.* London: Continuum, pp. 19–32.

Ovid. (2017). *Ovid's Heroides: A New Translation and Critical Essays.* Translated by Paul Murgatroyd, Sarah Parker and Bridget Reeves. London: Routledge.

Pacheco Aguilar, R. and Guénette, M.-F. (2021). *Situatedness and Performativity: Translation and Interpreting Practice Revisited.* Leuven: Leuven University Press.

Pietrzak, P. (2019). Scaffolding Student Self-Reflection in Translator Training. *Translation and Interpreting Studies* 14(3), 416–36.

Pint, K. and Ulldemolins, M. G. (2020). Roland Barthes and the 'Affective Truths' of Autotheory. *Mosaic: An Interdisciplinary Critical Journal* 53(4), 117–32. https://link.gale.com/apps/doc/A681135396/AONE?u=unilanc& sid=bookmark-AONE&xid=8021010a.

Pollock, D. (1998). Performing Writing. In P. Phelan and J. Lane, eds., *The Ends of Performance*. New York, NY: New York University Press, pp. 73–103.

Pollock, D. (2007). The Performative 'I'. *Cultural Studies Critical Methodologies* 7(10), 239–55.

Pratt, M. L. (1991). Arts of the Contact Zone. *Profession*, 33–40.

Preciado, P. (2008/2013). *Testo Junkie: Sex, Drugs, and Biopolitics in the Pharmacopornographic Era*. Translated by Bruce Benderson. New York, NY: Feminist Press.

Pushkin, N. (1825–1832/2018). *Eugene Onegin: A Novel in Verse: Text (Vol. 1)*. Translated by Vladimir Nabokov. Princeton, NJ: Princeton University Press.

Pym, A. (2014). *Method in Translation History*. London: Routledge.

Rancière, J. (2014). *The Politics of Aesthetics: The Distribution of the Sensible*. Translated by Gabriel Rockhill. New York, NY: Continuum.

Rehn, A. (2011). *Dangerous Ideas: When Provocative Thinking Becomes Your Most Valuable Asset*. Singapore: Marshall Cavendish.

Reynolds, M. (ed.) (2010). *The Sappho Companion*. London: Random House.

Robert-Foley, L. (2020). The Politics of Experimental Translation: Potentialities and Preoccupations. *English: Journal of the English Association* 69(267), 401–19.

Robert-Foley, L. (in press). *Experimental Translation: The Work of Translation in the Age of Algorithmic Production*. London: Goldsmith Press.

Robinson, D. (1991). *The Translator's Turn*. Baltimore, MD: John Hopkins University Press.

Robinson, D. (2022). *The Experimental Translator*. Cham: Palgrave Macmillan.

Rogoff, I. and Stiegler, B. (2010). Transindividuation. *E-Flux* 14. www.e-flux .com/journal/14/61314/transindividuation/.

Rossi, C. (2018). Translation as a Creative Force. In S. A. Harding, eds., *The Routledge Handbook of Translation and Culture*. London: Routledge, pp. 381–97.

Sakai, N. (2009). How Do We Count a Language? Translation and Discontinuity. *Translation Studies* 2(1), 71–88.

Sakai, N. (2017). The Modern Regime of Translation and the Emergence of the Nation. *The Eighteenth Century* 58(1), 105–8.

Salter, B. (2018). When Intellectuals Fail? Brexit and Hegemonic Challenge. *Competition & Change* 22(5), 467–87.

Samoyault, T. (2020). *Traduction et Violence*. Paris: Fiction & Cie.

Samuels, L. (2018). The Right to Be Transplace. In Á. Lehóczky and J. T. Welsch, eds., *Wretched Strangers*. London: Boiler House Press, pp. 238–41.

Samuels, L. and VanHove, H. (2020). Transplace Poetics: A Conversation and Reading with Lisa Samuels. *Journal for Literary and Intermedial Crossings* 5(2), i1–18.

Sappho. (1958/2019). *Sappho: A New Translation*. Translated by Mary Barnard. Oakland, CA: University of California Press.

Sappho. (2019). Fragment 55. Translated by Chris Childers. *Literary Matters* 12(1). www.literarymatters.org/12-1-sappho-55/.

Schäffner, C. (ed.) (1999). *Translation and Norms*. Bristol: Multilingual Matters.

Scott, C. (2012). *Literary Translation and the Rediscovery of Reading*. Cambridge: Cambridge University Press.

Scott, C. (2021). Developing Creative Models of Mind by 'Translational' Practice: From Critical to Creative Translation. In F. Mussgnug, M. Nabugodi and T. Petrou, eds., *Thinking through Relation: Encounters in Creative Critical Writing*. Oxford: Peter Lang, pp. 187–207.

Siddiqi, A. M. (2022). Preserving the Tender Things. In K. Bhanot and J. Tiang, eds., *Violent Phenomena: 21 Essays on Translation*. London: Tilted Axis Press, pp. 83–102.

Simon, S. (2019). *Translation Sites, A Field Guide*. London: Routledge.

Slavs and Tatars. (2015). *Satire in the Muslim World: Molla Nasreddin*. Recorded Public Lecture at NYU Abu Dhabi Institute. www.youtube.com/watch?v=0gzDXLih0rM.

Slavs and Tatars. (2017). *Molla Nasreddin: Polemics, Caricatures & Satires*. London: I. B. Tauris.

Snell-Hornby, M. (2006). *The Turns of Translation Studies: New Paradigms or Shifting Viewpoints?* Amsterdam: John Benjamins.

Sontag, S. (1981). *Against Interpretation and Other Essays*. New York, NY: Delta Book.

Spivak, G. (1993). *Outside in the Teaching Machine*. London: Routledge.

Stewart, K. (2008). Weak Theory in an Unfinished World. *Journal of Folklore Research* 45(1), 71–82.

Stiegler, B. (2013). Interobjectivity and Transindividuation. *Open! Platform for Art, Culture and the Public Domain* 28. https://onlineopen.org/interobjectivity-and-transindividuation.

Tahir Gürçağlar, Ş. (2002). What Texts Don't Tell: The Use of Paratexts in Translation Research. *Crosscultural Transgressions: Research Models in Translation Studies* 2, 44–60.

Tawada, Y. (2013). *Portrait of a Tongue: An Experimental Translation by Chantal Wright.* Translation and commentary by Chantal Wright. Ottawa: University of Ottawa Press.

Thomson, D. F. S. (1997). *Catullus: Edited with a Textual and Interpretative Commentary.* Translated by Douglas F. S. Thomson. Toronto: University of Toronto Press.

Toury, G. (1995). *Descriptive Translation Studies: And Beyond.* Amsterdam: John Benjamins.

Vandepitte, S. (2008). Remapping Translation Studies: Towards a Translation Studies Ontology. *Meta* 53(3), 569–88.

van Doorslaer, L. (2007). Risking Conceptual Maps. In Y. Gambier and L. van Doorslaer, eds., *The Metalanguage of Translation*, special issue of *Target* 19(2), 217–33.

Venuti, L. (2019). *Contra Instrumentalism: A Translation Polemic.* Lincoln: University of Nebraska Press.

Vidal Claramonte, Á. (2022). *Translation and Contemporary Art: Transdisciplinary Encounters.* New York, NY: Routledge.

Walkowitz, R. L. (2015). *Born Translated: The Contemporary Novel in an Age of World Literature.* New York, NY: Columbia University Press.

Wilson, E. (2004). Tongue Breaks. *London Review of Books* 26 (1). https://www.lrb.co.uk/the-paper/v26/n01/emily-wilson/tongue-breaks

Wittig, M. and Zeig, S. (1979). *Lesbian Peoples: Materials for a Dictionary.* London: Avon.

Yildiz, Y. (2013). *Beyond the Mother Tongue: The Postmonolingual Condition.* New York, NY: Fordham University Press.

Acknowledgements

This work is the product of many encounters, both intellectual and artistic. I think of it as a busy crossroad not only between fields of research but also between artists and scholars with whom I have exchanged on the subject of translation or whose works have inspired me over the years. My first and loving thanks goes to my husband, whose support and kindness have helped me throughout the most difficult parts of writing of this project. I also wish to thank my daughters, Elsie and Gabrielle, for their patience and caring encouragement. My parents and my sister, for their help with childcare and for cheering me on. I thank all members of the (D)raft writing group for their support and for reading part of this work while it was in progress: Sarah Jackson, Maria Gill Ulldemolins, Hannah Van Hove and Helena Hunter. The continuous exchanges of ideas and support which characterise our (para)academic writing group has been key in allowing me to think and imagine a different form and practice of scholarship. My thanks also go to Nicola Frith and Lily Robert-Foley, for their encouragements, shared writing sessions and intellectual solidarity throughout. Warm thanks also go to Timothy Mathews and Theo Hermans for their advice and support, and to Martha Harwood for allowing me to quote her final-year dissertation. I would also like to acknowledge the financial support I have received from MEITS/AHRC in order to conduct some of the practice-based research which is included in the last chapter, and to thank all the artists and translators who allowed me to reproduce their visual works. Finally, thank you to Kirsten Malmkjær for her patient support and advice throughout the writing and editing of this Element.

Cambridge Elements ≡

Translation and Interpreting

The series is edited by Kirsten Malmkjær with Sabine Braun as associate editor for Elements focusing on Interpreting.

Kirsten Malmkjær
University of Leicester

Kirsten Malmkjær is Professor Emeritus of Translation Studies at the University of Leicester. She has taught Translation Studies at the universities of Birmingham, Cambridge, Middlesex and Leicester and has written extensively on aspects of both the theory and practice of the discipline. *Translation and Creativity* (London: Routledge) was published in 2020 and *The Cambridge Handbook of Translation*, which she edited, was published in 2022. She is preparing a volume entitled *Introducing Translation* for the Cambridge Introductions to Language and Linguistics series.

Editorial Board

About the Series
Elements in Translation and Interpreting present cutting edge studies on the theory, practice and pedagogy of translation and interpreting. The series also features work on machine learning and AI, and human-machine interaction, exploring how they relate to multilingual societies with varying communication and accessibility needs, as well as text-focused research.

Cambridge Elements $\equiv$

Translation and Interpreting

Elements in the Series

Printed in the United States
by Baker & Taylor Publisher Services